"We all know whathe kind of lonely something very few has. In *Blueprint fo* the hardship and the hope of God's design for us to belong, and how each of us can find it."

Kadi Cole, leadership consultant, executive coach, and author of *Developing Female Leaders*. KadiCole.com

Praise for *How to Stay Standing*

"Alli Patterson's contagious joy and generous spirit make her a trusted guide."

Lisa Harper, speaker, Bible teacher, and bestselling author of *Life 100 Day Devotional*

"I know few people who have as much infectious joy about all things Bible as Alli."

Brian Tome, founding and senior pastor of Crossroads Church, author, and host of *The Aggressive Life* podcast

"Her authenticity, understanding, and knowledge of the Word will forever change your life."

Richard and Brittni De La Mora, founders of LoveAlwaysMinistries.com

"Alli has a way of writing that makes you stop and want *more* of God."

Amy Seiffert, speaker and author of *Starved* and *Grace Looks Amazing on You*

"Discipleship doesn't have to be fancy to be firm, and Alli charts a path which everyone everywhere can put into practice."

Bronwyn Lea, pastor and author of *Beyond Awkward Side Hugs*

BLUEPRINT
FOR
BELONGING

BLUEPRINT
FOR
BELONGING

The 5 Relationships Jesus Needed and Why You Need Them Too

ALLI PATTERSON

a division of Baker Publishing Group
Grand Rapids, Michigan

© 2025 by Alli Patterson

Published by Revell
a division of Baker Publishing Group
Grand Rapids, Michigan
RevellBooks.com

Printed in the United States of America

All rights reserved. No part of this publication may be reproduced, stored in a retrieval system, or transmitted in any form or by any means—for example, electronic, photocopy, recording—without the prior written permission of the publisher. The only exception is brief quotations in printed reviews.

Library of Congress Cataloging-in-Publication Data
Names: Patterson, Alli, 1977– author.
Title: Blueprint for belonging : the 5 relationships Jesus needed and why you need them too / Alli Patterson.
Description: Grand Rapids, Michigan : Revell, a division of Baker Publishing Group, [2025]
Identifiers: LCCN 2024014223 | ISBN 9780800742331 (paperback) | ISBN 9780800746803 (casebound) | ISBN 9781493448692 (ebook)
Subjects: LCSH: Spiritual formation. | Fellowship—Religious aspects—Christianity. | Jesus Christ—Example.
Classification: LCC BV4511 .P375 2025 | DDC 248.4—dc23/eng/20240513
LC record available at https://lccn.loc.gov/2024014223

Unless otherwise indicated, Scripture quotations are from the Holy Bible, New International Version®, NIV®. Copyright © 1973, 1978, 1984, 2011 by Biblica, Inc.® Used by permission of Zondervan. All rights reserved worldwide. www.zondervan.com. The "NIV" and "New International Version" are trademarks registered in the United States Patent and Trademark Office by Biblica, Inc.®

Scripture quotations labeled MSG are from The Message. Copyright © 1993, 2002, 2018 by Eugene H. Peterson. Used by permission of NavPress. All rights reserved. Represented by Tyndale House Publishers.

Scripture quotations labeled NET are from the NET Bible®. Copyright © 1996, 2019 by Biblical Studies Press, L.L.C. http://netbible.com. Used by permission. All rights reserved.

Illustrations by David Valentine

The author is represented by Alive Literary Agency, www.aliveliterary.com.

Baker Publishing Group publications use paper produced from sustainable forestry practices and postconsumer waste whenever possible.

25 26 27 28 29 30 31   7 6 5 4 3 2 1

To Bill, Andrew, Luke, Zoe, and Hope:
I love the place of belonging we have created together.

CONTENTS

INTRODUCTION

Living Lonely

I remember sitting at a table in my little black dress, watching the women around me laugh and talk, some '90s rap and a few friends nearby begging me to come to the dance floor. My date at the formal event that night had been my boyfriend for three years and we had just gotten engaged. I was by no means *alone*, but all these years later I still remember the hollow, empty sensation I felt inside. I was watching the evening happen around me, wondering if anyone else ever felt like I did in this crowd. I was invited. I belonged there, but I felt utterly and completely alone. Since we were on a boat, I had to stay a few more hours, but when I walked down the dock, I felt a wave of relief. I was hoping whatever triggered the tide of loneliness that came in that night would leave just as quickly. Until recently, I didn't understand why *that* situation with *those* people made me feel so terribly alone.

Humans have never felt more alone than we feel right now. Strangely, this is during an era when we have also never had a greater ability to stay connected. We are far more connected through our phones and social media than through the world of email and BlackBerrys that I had access to that night of the party on the boat. Yet loneliness now tops the list of mental and physical health crises for millions across the globe, with some nations even declaring it a new kind of epidemic. To me, this is clear evidence that the way we are pursuing relationships just isn't working for us. Our relational worlds aren't satisfying our basic human need for a secure sense of belonging and connection. We are living life far too lonely.

Loneliness is misalignment between the type of connections we *have* and the type we *need* for a thriving life. Human beings were intentionally designed by God to need and receive much of what makes a thriving life—first from him and then from other people. I'm not talking about external needs like work or food or transportation (though of course people are involved in those needs as well!), but rather our *internal* need to feel loved and connected, the sense that we belong somewhere, with someone. When that's missing, we walk through life feeling alone even if there are people everywhere we look.

Every one of us is designed to experience relationships where we feel **known**, **included**, **encouraged**, **welcomed**, and **expectant**. The roots of all five of these types of relationships start in our connection with God and take shape in and through our human relationships. When we live without the relationships we need, our souls are not fully satisfied: we're lonely. Most of us have probably learned to live this way, and it's been a long time since we felt the warmth and benefit of all five of these aspects of human connection. We all struggle sometimes to shake off the feeling that, when it comes right down to it, we are alone.

The head-scratching thing about loneliness is that everyone's experience of it is a little bit different. Most of us can't even explain *why* we feel lonely at certain times, like when I was at that party and surrounded by friends. Loneliness doesn't necessarily go away just because you have a few decent relationships in your life. The feeling creeps back in, creating days or even seasons when you might struggle to hear anything but the echo of the still-empty places in your life.

One type of relationship isn't meant to satisfy all your various needs for a sense of belonging. Just because you have a best friend doesn't mean you don't need the encouragement of people on the same life mission. Just because you have an extended family who loves you doesn't mean you don't need a group who will invite you to their BBQs. Just because you have a great work team doesn't mean you wouldn't welcome someone offering a new challenge in your life. One type of relationship that's working well just isn't enough, and neither is two or three. You are designed for all five!

A design for the variety of human relationships we need is found in the life of Jesus. His relational world contains a *blueprint of connection*. He walked through life unlike any other person, connected to the Father and operating in *five different types of relationships* that are part of meeting our deepest needs for human belonging. There are observable patterns to the priorities and tendencies he showed with each of these groups. I've combed through every single relationship that is recorded in the life of Jesus during his thirty-three years on earth and have found some fascinating patterns. He worked, connected, loved, and opened himself up differently in each space. Even though he, too, felt pain in this world, he put his relationships together in a way that resulted in thriving human bonds. The design of his relational world meant he lived far less lonely than we do in our more modern, "connected" world. As I uncovered this blueprint in the life of Christ and laid it on top of my own relational world, I found some pretty big holes in mine. And what's even more interesting is that these missing connections were linked to the very times and places in my life where I tended to feel the most alone. Could it be that the depth and design of each layer of our relational worlds are linked to the specific kinds of loneliness we each experience?

I've been looking for ways to pursue my missing connections because I believe that God wants more for me. I believe he wants to help me connect more deeply to other people because it's part of his design for human life. As I began to overlay this blueprint from Jesus onto my own life, it provided new insights for the strongest relationships in my life and also helped explain part of my long-standing discomfort in my family of origin. It became a new lens through which to view all the connections in my life. This blueprint empowered me to begin creating something new, and I started to take baby steps toward what I hope will be a long-term redesign of my relational world. I decided not to accept the idea that I would always feel a little bit lonely.

Most of us haven't really thought about the "why" and "how" behind the way we approach our relationships. I'm guessing you haven't arranged them in your life according to any real design. Most of us have simply collected family and friends over time, trying to hold on to them as best we can as the years go by. You may never have imagined there would be a way to bring order and intention to the haphazard way these connections are shaped, or that whether you do so may affect your own struggle with loneliness. After observing the life of Jesus, I'm convinced there is a strong connection. God wants you to experience a thriving life and fewer waves of loneliness. I believe he left help in the life of his Son. As you pattern your life after Christ in any significant way, you begin to live more fully alive. The way you pursue relationships is no different.

This book could be the beginning of a relational redesign of your life, but it won't be the end. I hope it will bring you some new language, some insight from Scripture, and some ways to begin a provocative discussion with God about which connections bring life, which ones you need to relocate, and which ones might not be as real as they look. You'll have to walk this path far beyond the blueprint presented in this book because relationships are a long and messy business. That's the reason I almost didn't write this book: it sounded like a topic for someone with more ideal relationships in their life. If there is such a thing as a relationship expert, I'm certainly not it. I can think of much better counselors and much better friends. However, I couldn't look away from the biggest heartache in our culture today, not when I knew the life of Jesus could offer a glimmer of help and hope.

Loneliness is the built-in alarm that something isn't relationally right in our lives. It's getting louder, and many people are taking notice. In May 2023, US Surgeon General Dr. Vivek Murthy issued a warning that the long-term impact of loneliness on one's health is the equivalent of smoking fifteen cigarettes per day. He said, "Our relationships are a source of healing and well-being hiding in plain sight—one that can help us live healthier, more fulfilled, and more productive lives."[1]

1. U.S. Department of Health and Human Services, "New Surgeon General Advisory Raises Alarm about the Devastating Impact of the Epidemic of Loneliness and Isolation in the United States," May 3, 2023, https://www.hhs.gov /about/news/2023/05/03/new-surgeon-general-advisory-raises-alarm-about-deva stating-impact-epidemic-loneliness-isolation-united-states.html.

I agree that the secret to living less lonely is hidden inside our relationships. But the report goes on to outline six pillars of what the government will do to fix this problem. A government might be able to reconstruct neighborhoods and health-care systems, but it cannot solve the aches of a human heart. It cannot change our motives in the way we pursue our family and friends. Health-care policies, new urban housing plans, extra playgrounds, and online habits may be things a government can design, but there is a God who designed you as a whole soul and has the keys to your thriving. The first step toward a life of greater connection is acknowledging his design and considering where and how you are living outside of it. Come with me on this journey into the relational world of Jesus to witness the layers of relationships in his life. Along the way, my hope is for you to discover the first step toward greater belonging and away from whatever kind of loneliness you feel today. You were designed by a God who loves you and wants you to live feeling known, included, encouraged, welcomed, and expectant. And much, much less lonely.

The Life of a Soul

Then the LORD God formed a man from the dust of the ground and breathed into his nostrils the breath of life, and the man became a living being.

Genesis 2:7

My great-aunt Flo studied everyone's breasts. Florence had a reputation in the family for walking up to female relatives and asking, "Are those real?" Exactly zero women in my family have breast implants, so no one can quite account for this preoccupation. Young or old, large or small, you could be sure that Flo would be at every family wedding or holiday in her push-up bra, staring at what was in yours. Flo was convinced the real ones had a certain shape, a certain way they moved, a certain density. If she wasn't sure about yours, she looked and watched and evaluated . . . and eventually just asked. It was possible that your answer might be followed up with questions about whether there was something stuffed inside your bra. I learned early on to steer clear of her at family events—or at least to wear something loose fitting. If I were putting it nicely, I'd say she was a "character." Flo certainly left us a lot of family stories for Thanksgiving.

What you are going to do in this book is a bit like what Flo did. You are going to stare intently at something that's hard to see clearly: the life of your soul. You are going to wonder and ask questions about the form, shape, and density of what can seem invisible. You are going to ask about empty places on the inside and how they connect to relationships on the outside. You are going to bravely consider if you might be living with a less thriving soul than you could have. But what even *is* a soul? How do you evaluate the health and form of something that's hard to put into words or see?

Or is it?

I used to think of my soul and my body as two completely different things: my body was just a bag of bones, and my soul was the thing inside it that flies off to heaven when I die. I am a linear thinker, so clean categories like this appeal to me. I used to draw harder lines between the pieces of me that are visible and those that are invisible. However, the more I live life and read Scripture, the less these firmly separated categories make sense to me. The picture of humanity in the Bible isn't so sharply divided between body and soul. Rather, it's a picture of a beautifully integrated creation. The biblical idea of a soul isn't something you possess inside a body: it's what you *are*. You are a soul. You are an integrated, whole, embodied human soul who is alive because of the life force that the Bible calls *ruach*—the Hebrew word for spirit or breath. So you are an embodied soul animated by an invisible life-breath of spirit.

The Hebrew word for soul is *nephesh*, and it's often translated into English as simply "I" or "me." The use of the English word "soul" to translate *nephesh* was an unfortunate choice because our instinctive thoughts about what a soul is have been influenced more by Greek philosophy than the Bible. It's easy to misunderstand places where the Bible talks about the soul and think it's Plato's or Aristotle's version of it. Those philosophers trained us to think of the material world we live in as an inferior shadow of a higher, immaterial reality. The implications of Greek philosophy permeate our culture today. You can hear it when people talk of the soul as if it is the "real you" trapped inside your physical existence. We have come to speak of the soul as something separate and of a higher order, inevitably leading us to put a lower value on the body. Today I hear talk about the body as something that "gets in the way" of your real, spiritual self, which exists as your soul. We have come to think of our soul as our ideal, true (and disembodied) existence that is perfected after death when we are released from this cage of flesh. This is absolutely not the picture we get in Scripture of humanity's design! And it leads us to overlook the very real ways our external and internal senses of health and wholeness are integrated.

In reality, you were formed carefully and purposefully, body and soul together, so I prefer to refer to you and me as "embodied souls." The Bible indicates that God's design for humanity is an integrated external and internal life. About the only place in our culture where I still hear the word *soul* used anywhere close to this idea is when an airplane crashes. Pilots still count the number of "souls on board," which is a relic of an old proper English usage of the word *soul*. (That's probably why that word was chosen in biblical translation to begin with!) If there were 137 "souls on board" when the plane went down, then there were 137 complete, valuable, precious humans lost.

If your physical flesh is not a meaningless shell inside which your *nephesh* is trapped, this means your life is fully integrated—the external way you live has everything to do with the well-being of your mind, emotions, and will.

We all experience the truth of this every single day. Whatever is happening in your mind directly affects your physicality. Your passions and emotions pulsing through your "heart" can be seen in changes of your skin color (blushing, getting red with anger, paling with worry). When I first began to teach in front of thousands of people, I felt the anxiety in my digestive system: it wasn't unusual to make extra trips to the bathroom. I learned to eat only certain things on Sunday mornings. I also recall all the weight I lost during the era when my marriage was in trouble: I had no appetite for weeks upon weeks over my worry, sadness, and fear for our future. I can still describe the gray plaid pants that had always been too tight but started hanging loosely on my frame because of all the emotional turmoil. Your visible, external body responds as though it's connected to your invisible, internal state—because it is. How many doctors tell their patients to reduce an intangible thing like stress in order to preserve their very tangible heart? How many eating disorder patients come to understand their struggle with their body begins in beliefs lurking in their hearts and minds? Our bodies are not separate from what happens in our mind, our will, and our emotions. You know this already from living life as a human soul. There is no doubt that you are one created being—tangible and intangible, physical and spiritual. Our bodies and souls are inseparable in their original intent and design.

There is one very specific question that can quickly get you to a good assessment of the state of your whole soul. The answer is indicative of so many things in your life that are both visible and invisible. Much of what goes on in your heart, mind, and emotions depends on this, and it is deeply connected to the way you live your physical life every day. There's one question you have to be brave enough to ask and reflective enough to answer in this book. It's one that often indicates the overall health of you as a whole soul, and it might surprise you.

How deeply and how often do you feel lonely?

Loneliness is the cry of a soul that is made for and fed by something very specific. There is something external we all need, and its presence or absence has an impact on the overall state of our internal mind, heart, will, and emotions. When you hear and feel this deep silent cry of loneliness, it is a cry for something you need in your real, flesh and blood life. There is one aspect of your life where the visible and invisible may be most deeply intertwined.

Your relationships.

Relationships consume your mind, will, and emotions— and they are also lived out externally every single day. The state of your relationships is nearly always a fair assessment of your state as a human soul.

If you want more life from the inside out, you have to look closely at how you're doing relationships. So throughout the book you are going to look at every single one of them. I want you to think about the friendships, family relationships, and human connections—big or small, present or past—that are affecting your life from the inside out. The design of your relational world matters more to the thriving of your life than any other single factor.

Relationships: God's Design

Genesis 1 in the Bible is where we can find the account of God creating life in all its different forms. He created varieties of plants and animals and spaces for them to thrive, grow, and reproduce. He called all his creation good. Then he made a human being, and Genesis 2 is an up-close look at this unique, final creation of life. Strangely, unlike all the other parts of creation, God wasn't completely satisfied with what he had made. This is the first time in Scripture we find the word *alone*: God declared that "it is not good for the man to be alone" (Gen. 2:18). Adam, the first human, had breath in his lungs, a beautiful place to live, a job to do, and delicious food to eat, but he existed in some kind of state that could only be remedied by another of his kind. God's displeasure with Adam's loneliness means those other things by themselves were not, according to God's original design for Adam, going to fulfill him. For the thriving, growth, satisfaction, and reproduction of human beings, the external blessings of the world were not the answer to this dissatisfactory state of being "alone."

God created us to live and thrive in the context of *relationship*. Human life is designed not just for the physical body and physical world, but for existence in a state of *connection*. God wanted Adam to feel a sense of deep belonging in the world he'd created. Beyond Genesis, even a simple observation of human life would verify that thriving depends upon connection. There was a moment at each of my four children's births when I said something like, "It's so nice to finally meet you," because the birth of a human life is the birth of a *relationship*. Their new life depended upon a healthy bond with *me* for their thriving. Though each of my kids was uniquely made in the image of God with individual value, none of them could have survived without me—and not just physically. When I became a mom, I realized that I was being entrusted with shaping four souls that God made, inside and out. He connected us for that very purpose.

When I had kids, my bank account got smaller, my car got bigger, my vacations got less interesting, and I got used to being followed into the bathroom. However, it was motherhood that taught me firsthand the power of human connection to reshape someone's inner being. It taught me the life-shaping power of living inside a strong sense of belonging. Having a child is the most condensed example I can think of to demonstrate how we morph and change with the creation and dissolution of relationships. Even if you aren't a parent, you have one, so you know the power of being shaped and reshaped by people in your life. At the beginning of your life, the terrain of your soul was shaped by your parents' or caretakers' capacities, their degree of steadiness or anxiety, their neglect or presence, their favorite pastimes and activities, their intellectual curiosity, and their ideas of risk and caution. For better or for worse, the elements, depth, and makeup of your internal state and your external thriving depended upon your earliest connections. Your soul took on a certain "shape" because of the people around you.

Each human is created and shaped materially and immaterially by relationships. God designed human souls to be moldable, vulnerable, and permeable to the connections around us. This is not some sort of weird codependency;

it's part of our divine design so that we live with the sense that we belong to God and to others—exactly the state that God intended for Adam's life.

Unfortunately, modern Western culture has increasingly lost sight of this design. We tend to prioritize the accumulation of experiences and possessions—the very ones God knew from the beginning weren't going to satisfy us when we felt alone! We often prioritize these things over finding the greater sense of belonging *with people*. We regularly move away from long-standing friendships to pursue jobs. We cut off family connections to have more adventures or make more money. And the basic practices that connect us to others in quality, meaningful ways are being traded for more shallow habits that seem like an easier version of the "same thing." Instead of meeting up with friends to talk face-to-face, we text. Instead of crossing the city to have dinner together, we both sit alone with our phones and post pictures of our food. Instead of meeting in person, we work on Zoom. We increasingly act out an underlying belief that the place where we live, the job we do, and the food we eat are what will satisfy our thirst for a deeper, better life. We go in search of a soul-satisfying life in these places.

However, God looked at all those good things that he had made in the beginning and said, "That'll never be enough to satisfy a human." *Relationships* are the only things that create fullness of life for the human soul. Money, accomplishment, travel, indulgence, physical perfection—the types of things most people spend their lives trying to obtain—will never sustain our inner life to the same extent. I wonder how our lives would change if we pursued the right set of relationships with the same intention and vigor we put into getting all of those other things. Jesus warned us to keep an eye on our inner life first because he said it's entirely possible that we could search for life on the outside, focused exclusively on things that we think will benefit our body or material existence (think jobs and gyms and bank accounts)—and in doing so lose our very life.

I accidentally verified this truth a few summers ago. I was stepping into a new industry and onto a steep professional learning curve. I wanted to succeed. I wanted my first project to go well. By the end of the summer, I'd done just about everything I could to ensure a satisfying result—researching, meeting with consultants, creating new ideas, working extra hours—only to look around and realize that, despite my great work, I was unhappy and stressed. I felt disconnected from nearly everyone I loved. I was worse off for it. I felt like a fool for falling into what

> God looked at all those good things that he had made in the beginning and said, "That'll never be enough to satisfy a human." *Relationships are the only things that create fullness of life for the human soul.*

was, when I stepped back and looked, a tale as old as time. Work was going well, but I felt less alive and less satisfied from the inside out. I made a bad trade looking for a better life. Jesus warned about this kind of foolish trade-off when he said, "What good is it for someone to gain the whole world, yet forfeit their soul? Or what can anyone give in exchange for their soul?" (Mark 8:36–37). He thought the keeping of your soul—the essence of life in your inner being—was of crucial importance. I hope you'll soon become convinced that you, as a soul, are formed and satisfied only with layers and varieties of certain relationships that are worth sacrificing other things to keep healthy. I've decided I need a sticky note on my bathroom mirror that says:

Alli,
what good is it
for you to gain
the whole world,
yet forfeit your
<u>relationships</u>?

I am way too quick to trade them for other things. The wide variety of types and depths and aches of loneliness tells you that you were designed for a corresponding variety of types and depths of human connection. When one of those is broken or missing, you feel that nagging, hollow feeling that you're missing out on something vital to your life. The fact that we have a word for this odd internal experience of "alone-ness" is testimony to an intentional *design*.

The problem is not what God designed in Genesis 1 and 2, it's what happened in Genesis 3. Sin entered the original creation. Sin affects all our relationships, the same ones we depend on for receiving what we need to thrive. Every one of us intuitively understands the negative impact of devalued, broken, or missing human connections that weren't fully what we needed. Even today when someone asks you, "How are you doing?" the deepest answer is almost always found in an assessment of your relational world. You—an embodied human soul—are doing about as well as your relationships are doing. The invisible impact of damaged relationships has wreaked havoc in all our lives in very real and visible ways. I know you've lived the truth that the less healthy your relationships are, the more you suffer from the inside out. What I want you to fully embrace is *the design underneath that truth*. God has a design for your relational world, and he left us a blueprint for it.

Even if this world of sin prevents you from ever living that design perfectly and fully, any steps you take in that direction will certainly mean a richer, more satisfying life. You, as a soul, are relational at your very core. Nothing influences your mind, will, emotions—your internal "terrain"—as formationally as the real people around you. Every person is built into a different shape because of relationships. Your thriving and wholeness as a soul are determined almost entirely by the various human bonds established and experienced throughout your life.

God intends for you to soak up and soak in all kinds of nourishment and life from him *and* from the people around you. We were all made to affect the well-being of the souls around us. God's amazing design for human life is one that depends upon invisible *connection* of human souls to create thriving. When your connections are well-formed and growing, your relational world takes on a dense, authentic, thicker, layered quality, creating a certain "shape" on the outside that leads to health on the inside. You are about to explore that shape in blueprint form.

First, I want you to consider your current state. Be Aunt Flo for a moment. What shape are you in as a human soul?

The first way to take an honest look at that is to consider our key question.

How deeply and how often do you feel lonely?

Everybody, no matter the language, culture, or era, understands the kind of emptiness that echoes in an invisible place inside when they feel disconnected. Loneliness is a deeply shared and yet oddly individual experience. Sometimes it's as fleeting as a song I hear on a random Spotify playlist, and other times it's a stubborn presence that won't leave no matter where I go. I have felt loneliness as a passing ache for someone who used to be closer, or as a wave that rolls in as soon as I drive to a certain spot. In some seasons of life it has felt like a hopeless sadness constantly whispering that "I don't have any real friends" or "No one really knows me." Today I felt a little stab of it as I drove home after a run. A sudden sense of loneliness came over me at the thought of my firstborn leaving for college in a few months. Even when he's standing in front of me, I miss him already. Loneliness can take on all these different forms because we are complex, designed souls that influence one another's thriving. We don't need just physical health but also specific kinds of relationships for flourishing life as a human soul. Because we are one whole being created with connection from the inside out, our internal experience of loneliness is deeply connected to the design of our relationships.

We need a wake-up call to remember how God designed true, rich human connection—and return to a pursuit of what is good for human souls. I have often been mistaken in what would bring me the fulfillment I long for. I have pushed away relationships for the sake of work. I have invested in the wrong relationships for the wrong reasons. I have taken too much or too little from others. I have avoided some relationships altogether because reconciliation is difficult. I've spent too much time worried about people who exist inside my devices but will never stand in front of me. I have suffered the outcome of all that in various kinds of loneliness because I never knew that God left me a blueprint for the life of my soul.

I found it in the relationships of Jesus.

The Relationships of Jesus

I always assumed that Jesus was lonely in the same ways that I am, but now I believe something a little different. He certainly knew pain and suffering in relationships, but the idea of *loneliness* in his life requires some nuance. Jesus certainly felt relational pain. He was rejected and misunderstood by others. He was betrayed and disobeyed by people. He sometimes had to stay by himself or avoid cities and places where he was threatened and unwelcome. There were certainly times he was alone—by necessity, mission, or choice. He was also alone in that he was a singular type of man in all of human history: the only begotten Son of God, made flesh.

So, yes, Jesus did experience a variety of ways he was unique or alone. However, I cannot find the words in Scripture to defend the idea that Jesus lived in the sort of loneliness that many of us do today—detached from the very essence of human life and deeply deprived of the need for connection. The one time I can find it is on the cross, the very lowest moment of his life. While we will never identify with the depth of physical and spiritual agony of that event, many people resonate with what Jesus cried out at his soul's most painful moment. He used David's words from Psalm 22:1, "My God, my God, why have you forsaken me?" Over and above the physical pain, those words seem to express a feeling of abandonment and loneliness that many of us feel deep inside and live with every day.

Jesus walked his days on earth very differently. He lived in deep connection to his Father, which led him to be a relationally well-formed man. Despite the pain he experienced in relationships, his soul was in good shape because he knew how to live life deeply and richly. He took seriously his connection with God and with other people. Jesus developed five realms of relationships in his earthly life. He created and maintained a **core, circle, comrades, community**, and **crowd**. Through this ecosystem of connection, he lived a thriving human life. Even Jesus needed all these relationships because he was not only fully God but fully man, living out the perfect design for human life. He developed best friends, worked alongside his disciples, received resources from others, and was built up by comrades on the same mission. He somehow managed to communicate deep love and commitment to the Jewish people while always welcoming outsiders and strangers in the crowds around him. He never once sinned. He always loved perfectly. He stayed on the mission his Father gave him. I'm tired just thinking about trying to do all this, let alone actually knowing how, when, and where to give and receive in all these different ways.

I always feel so limited in my relational capacity. This week I felt like a lousy friend when I had to cancel margaritas because of a back-to-school night. Last week I invested in professional relationships at a conference, and I missed things happening in my husband's life three time zones away. The time and resources it takes to be richly present to some always seems to shortchange others. Sometimes I'm okay with the trade-offs and priority calls I make, but other times

I second-guess myself or struggle with classic mom guilt, feeling like I never manage to give all four kids what they need at the same time. I feel frustratingly limited in who I can connect with in a twenty-four-hour day in one location. I make the wrong call or let someone down much more often than I wish. I never seem to master the art of holding on to "my people" and welcoming new ones with the same intentionality; when I foster some connections, other ones seem to suffer.

Jesus was limited in the same basic human ways we are. He lived within the confines of twenty-four-hour days, needed to get and prepare food, had to work and sleep, *and* needed to maintain the health of his invisible mind, heart, will, and emotions—which meant attending well to his relationships. Jesus was God, but a God who chose to empty himself of his limitless nature. Read that again: *Jesus emptied himself of his limitless nature* to come and embrace constraints like the ones you have. He *took on needs* he didn't previously have in his heavenly dwelling as the eternal Son of God. Jesus agreed to face competing requests for his time and a family who made demands and misunderstood him. He had to walk from place to place at about three miles per hour instead of enjoying the omnipresence previously available to him. Jesus lived a human life with many places he couldn't be and many people he couldn't see all at once. Do those kinds of limitations sound familiar?

However, Jesus also maintained the fullness of his soul through well-developed, real, deep relationships. He never made the wrong trades when it came to tasks versus people. He never let the wrong people in. He grew in the wisdom and understanding of how his Father designed relationships to work so his human soul was deeply satisfied. The richness of his inner life began with a deep connection to his Father, but it flourished because he lived fully within his Father's holistic design for humanity. That design necessitated giving and receiving through *relationships* what is needed for a thriving life. Jesus didn't circumvent that design because he was fully God; he lived squarely within it because he was fully man.

Jesus could do this because his everyday relational world had a *design*. Far from haphazard, Jesus had five critical types of relationships. The way he attended to them was out of an overflow from his center of connection to God, which allowed him to form, prioritize, and love all his human relationships in just the right way. (Something I can never manage to do.) Jesus's life was more beautiful, more intentional, and much less lonely than our lives feel. In each of his five realms of relationship, God provided for his needs to grow in wisdom, be attached and included, experience feeling truly known, and engage in the adventure and unscripted moments of human life. Jesus lived these just as we need to. Each of the five types of relationships included certain types of people who made his life rich and fruitful and authentically human. Each of the five types also had identifiable characteristics: specific natures of interaction, certain activities, and notable boundaries around time, intimacy, activity, or conversation. We desperately need this wisdom because Jesus lived fulfilled in a way that most of us do not.

As we search the relationships of Jesus together in each chapter, I hope you'll consider what these types of relationships look like for you, and whether Jesus may have been on to something in how he lived and related to others. I want you to blend this ancient wisdom with your modern world to see how you might be able to reshape your external relationships and as a result bring internal life to you as a soul. Some of the patterns we have learned from our culture today are failing us. Whenever you find a difference in how you think of people or relate to others versus how Jesus did (because you will), I believe you will also find the origin of your lonely moments— whether brief and fleeting or constant and dark. The life of Jesus gives hope for something beyond loneliness.

When I sat feeling lonely at the party I described in the introduction, I didn't have words to express that my sense of loneliness was coming from having chosen the wrong comrades. Early in college, despite being a Christian, I had rejected the gatherings of Campus Crusade for Christ (now called Cru), which was the main source for Christian friendships and fun on my campus. I told myself I just didn't vibe with them, and I joined a sorority instead. The party I described happened at the very end of my senior year. I was engaged to be married and I had friends. However, I was struggling with a kind of loneliness that a fiancé and friends do not address: a sense that I had attached myself to entirely the wrong group of people. We shared no mission. We shared no common goals. I had no interest in pursuing the objectives of sorority life any of the years I was in it. Despite meeting some lovely women, I had no true comrades, no one who fully shared my life direction, no one who knew my faith, no one who could fight alongside me toward any kind of kingdom mission. It was a costly mistake. Almost four years later, not only had my faith withered terribly, but I could not shake the sense that these people—no matter how nice—were not *my* people. I'd chosen the wrong comrades, and I felt alone.

You can't shake off that kind of loneliness. Now I see that. Now I understand the feelings I had that night. I could only walk away from the party in relief that it was the last of its kind. I had chosen badly for my network of relationships in college, and it cost me a piece of my soul. The potential friendships I rejected as a freshman took years to rebuild another way. I felt a lot more of the same kind of loneliness, but slowly God began to help me fix this aspect of loneliness in my life when I started to meet new people in my new city after graduation. God restored comrades to me in an almost laughable way. I actually met and became friends with a handful of people at my new church in Cincinnati, Ohio, who had been in Cru at my college during the very years I rejected that avenue of relationship. I felt God wink at me as though he were saying, "No worries. I brought you back to the right ones." The way God redesigned that realm of relationship in my life still makes me laugh.

You're about to take a hard look at your relational world and begin a relationship redesign inspired by the life of Jesus. God wants to develop, celebrate, or repair five different kinds of relationships in your life. Your inner self is being shaped by the state of them in your life today, and he wants more for you! These five are a unique blend of connections in which your whole soul—your very life—can truly thrive. I have spent plenty of hours looking in the mirror, wishing one of my body parts was a different shape, but I have never given much thought to what has shaped and formed me as a soul. Be Aunt Flo. Look hard. Ask questions. Be honest about what is real and not real. Let yourself feel and remember the loneliness. You may be surprised to see that God has actual, practical help to offer. There might be some relationships you need to push further out, some you need to double-down on, and others you simply need to name and clarify.

The Hebrew word *yakhid*, translated "lonely" ("only, singular"), comes from the root word *yakhad*, which is translated "to be united or joined." The word *lonely* is rooted in precisely the opposite of loneliness! *Yakhad* is the essence of a unified, joined *community that is one*, and *yakhid* is the individual who experiences a world of one—a world without the oneness of connection. As you go about this redesign, I want you to ask yourself, "Am I *yakhid* or *yakhad* in this realm of relationship?" As you examine your relationships closely, maybe you will find places you are *yakhad*—thriving in thick connections with others—and some places you are *yakhid* and your relational ties are too thin. These are bound to be the places in your life where you experience your own unique recipe of loneliness. Whatever you find to remodel, there is a God who can replace what's been missing, restore what's been wasted, and fix what's been broken.

Spend some time right now thinking of all the relationships in your life. Every single one. Do a good job, because you're going to use this later. Using your phone, social media, memory, or pictures, write down as many names as possible, in no particular order. Come back and add more as they pop into your head. After that, move on to a deep dive with me into each type of relationship in the life of Jesus. You're going to consider the blueprint of his life overlaid on your own. I pray you will see and follow the Lord into his unique, life-giving, redesigned shape of *you*: an integrated human soul.

tes • workout partners • teammates • family • uncles • cousins • neighbors • teammates •

coworkers • aunts • uncles • cousins • neighbors • bosses • school friends • roommates • family • friends • uncles • neighbors • teammates

y • friends • coworkers • aunts • family • friends • coworkers • workout partners • aunts •

Live Known by a Core

One who has unreliable friends soon comes to ruin,
but there is a friend who sticks closer than a brother.

Proverbs 18:24

We had a large porch addition put on the back of our house about two years ago. For a long time we'd felt too enclosed with no easy access to the outside. We would sit drinking coffee, saying things like, "Wouldn't it be great if the door was over *there* and there was a big porch *here*?" The extent of the redesign—tearing off the back of the kitchen and rebuilding most of the deck—had stopped us for years, but our desire to sit in the open air and feel a breeze while watching the Bengals on a fall Sunday afternoon got stronger and stronger. We could practically taste the coffee out there on a crisp morning.

To get to the finished product, we first needed a blueprint. Every redesign starts there. A builder must have an image with elements and measurements to know what and how they're trying to build. The blueprint offered to us for our relationships—the design you never even thought to ask for—is found in the life of Jesus. At the very first meeting for our porch project, we stood in the yard and translated the desires of our heart onto a piece of paper. Then we faced the reality of our current structure and discussed what steps, limitations, and options we had.

As you read through the description of each type of relationship in the life of Jesus, I want you to do the same: Tell God how you imagine your relational world could be, what you want more and less of. Then look together at your current structure and use the blueprint to build from wherever you are today to a life of deeper connection and belonging.

The first type of relationship on the blueprint of Jesus's life is his **core**. The core is made up of your irreplaceable few. For Jesus this was Peter, James, and John. These guys were likely the first people that others associated with him. They were his guys, his bros, his homies—the ones who were always allowed "in." Your core few are *the people of your people*, the ones who know you like no one else.

Human souls need to feel known to experience love. The extent to which you believe you're known by someone is the extent to which you will be able to feel loved by that person. Your core knows you—the *real* you—and loves you anyway, so they're in the best position to give you a vital sense of unconditional love. The commitment to love one another despite flaws and through pain and hardship is why your spouse is in your core if you are married. But core friends can see you and love you like that too. King David made a best friend like this early in his life, and in 1 Samuel 18:1 it says that "Jonathan became one in spirit with David, and he loved him as himself." These men shared a trust and lifelong pact to stay loyal to a friendship they both honored until the end of their lives.

There are a lot of unique aspects to the connection with your core few, but a sure sign of this type of connection is a great nickname. Nicknames signify a deep *knowing* and a sense of *belonging* together, which is why psychologists have observed that you are more likely to give the closest few people in your life a nickname than anyone else. My nickname tactic has always been to shorten them as much as humanly possible. My friend Amy, who was in my core for many years growing up, I just called "Aim." (Is that even really shortened?) My husband's college friends called him "Rubble." (Yep, a Flintstones reference of some kind.) Jesus called James and John "the sons of thunder" and called Simon "Peter," which means "Rock." None of his other disciples got a nickname. Nicknames aren't benign pet names; they signal the familiarity and belonging indicative of a core relationship, testifying to others this deep level of comfort or inside knowledge.

Core relationships are God's design to provide us with a flesh and blood experience of unconditional love—or as close as we can humanly get! Most of us are aware that we are flawed people, but our human instinct is to cover up the imperfections that we think might cause someone to reject us. God's design for human connection, however, works in an upside-down way: the risk to expose your real nature, your real dreams, and your real perspective—including all the flaws—leads to the experience of authentic belonging and connection. It's a short hop from there to love. Your flaws don't stop this at all! They act as a sort of guarantee that you are loved not because you're perfect but because you're *you*. The more you are known by someone and still accepted, the more you feel the deep sense that you belong with that person. This is precisely the kind of love God has for you. You, flaws and all, are invited into the deepest connection possible, through Jesus Christ. And your **core** is part of how you will grow to believe more and more that you belong to the God who initiated that kind of love.

Building Your Core

Jesus had ways of building his core relationships, and the most powerful one was **proactive self-disclosure**. If you want to strengthen relationships in and for a core, you need to watch for a chance to be vulnerable with that person and take it. For some of you this is second nature: you're an open book! Vulnerability isn't scary for you because the times you've put it all on the table, people have loved you anyway. But not everyone has had that experience. Some of you have been judged or canceled or abandoned, or you learned a long time ago not to expose your internal life to people around you because hurt was waiting for you there. Some people need a little warm-up and a *lot* of practice to reach a core level of vulnerability. If that's you, as you look at the blueprint of your relational world versus Jesus's, you may find some holes here or lots of room to deepen these connections. God wants to heal and fill you through a core so you can live less lonely.

Jesus's greatest act of self-disclosure was an event referred to as the transfiguration. The people he took with him into this situation were—you guessed it—Peter, James, and John. They got to see a part of Jesus that no one else on earth ever saw. If you have ever taken a friend to your hometown, introduced them to your parents, and let them see the room you grew up in, that might be a tiny whiff of what this experience was like. I once took my friend Amanda to my hometown with me, and she met my aunt who still calls me Allison, saw my dad's creative flair on a charcuterie board, and drank margaritas with my favorite cousin. It was a willing self-disclosure, and our relationship grew as a result. She saw pieces of me that helped her make better sense of who I was. She saw me as a daughter, a cousin, and a niece—parts of me our daily rhythms would never naturally afford her. Now I can skip the explanation when I want to arrange fresh flowers in a *very* specific way and just say, "You met my dad, right?"

I wonder if the transfiguration is an example of Jesus taking his friends home to meet some of his family—his Father, Moses, and Elijah. Jesus brought Peter, James, and John with him to a mountaintop and purposely left others out of it, showing them a part of his nature that no other humans witnessed.

> After six days Jesus took with him Peter, James and John the brother of James, and led them up a high mountain by themselves. There he was transfigured before them. His face shone like the sun, and his clothes became as white as the light. Just then there appeared before them Moses and Elijah, talking with Jesus.
>
> Peter said to Jesus, "Lord, it is good for us to be here. If you wish, I will put up three shelters—one for you, one for Moses and one for Elijah."

While he was still speaking, a bright cloud covered them, and a voice from the cloud said, "This is my Son, whom I love; with him I am well pleased. Listen to him!"

When the disciples heard this, they fell facedown to the ground, terrified. But Jesus came and touched them. "Get up," he said. "Don't be afraid." When they looked up, they saw no one except Jesus.

As they were coming down the mountain, Jesus instructed them, "Don't tell anyone what you have seen, until the Son of Man has been raised from the dead." (Matt. 17:1–9)

Jesus's core three witnessed his divinity that day. They saw some of the fullness of who he was. The verb used to describe what happened when his face shone and his clothes turned white was *metamorphoō*, which means to "transfigure," "transform," or "change in form"; in other words, **to make something internal become outwardly visible.** They witnessed his glory, and he purposely allowed them to see it. Jesus knew one day these three would be central in testifying to who he really was and what his life, death, and resurrection meant. So he let them *know him* in a deeper way, giving them a glimpse of his past, present, and future in his Father's kingdom. They heard his Father's words about him. They encountered other "friends" Jesus had. All of it confirmed who they'd come to believe he was: the Messiah, the fulfillment of both the Law (Moses) and the Prophets (Elijah).

Peter showed keen, heavenly insight about his friend just before this experience when Jesus asked him, "Who do you say I am?" (Matt. 16:15), and he proclaimed a belief that Jesus was the Messiah. But that insight needed rounding out, even correcting in some ways. That same day Peter had rebuked Jesus as Jesus prophesied his own death, Peter saying, "This shall never happen to you!" (Matt. 16:22). Peter needed a fuller, clearer picture of not only who Jesus was but also the work and mission of his life. The vulnerability of the transfiguration confirmed, clarified, and corrected this understanding so these three could see more of him.

How can you allow your core to see a new part of you? I challenge you to do it on purpose to deepen your connection. Take them with you to visit your aging parents, offer to pray for them when they tell you they're having a hard time, tell them what you really think of something—whatever is *not* something you'd typically expose of yourself or your life. Your core sees you, and they need to see *all* of you. God allows these unique few people a grace to understand you in a way that isn't clear to others. Their role is to speak life to the real you and to believe in your true identity until you believe it too. The moments you are vulnerable are the moments you give them permission to call you up and into who you truly are. You desperately need people who know and believe in you at this level. Your core is part of how God brings all of you to life.

Two people in my core each told me a long time ago they saw God was going to do a unique ministry through my life. One has consistently called me out anytime I have shrunk back from it. The other—my husband—always seems to have a sense of where God is taking me before I do. They've each provided important encouragement and even insistence for me to keep stepping into the life God has for me. When I don't believe, they do. If we disagree, I can handle the challenge because I am confident in their love. The ability to give and receive challenging and even chastening words is the mark of a good core connection.

If all you've ever heard is sweetness and affirmation from someone, speaking challenge may tell you if they're truly a part of your core.

> Wounds from a friend can be trusted,
> but an enemy multiplies kisses. (Prov. 27:6)

The other practice that builds your core is **allowing your needs to be met** through them. It's strange to think of other people meeting the needs of Jesus, the Son of God. But he had human needs and allowing others to meet those needs is part of what builds relationship. Jesus did this in Luke 22: "Jesus sent Peter and John, saying, 'Go and make preparations for us to eat the Passover'" (v. 8). He sent them to arrange critical plans for his final Passover. And a few days later, when he was hanging on a cross, Jesus counted on his core friend John to meet needs in a way that he could no longer meet them himself. "When Jesus saw his mother there, and the disciple whom he loved standing nearby, he said to her, 'Woman, here is your son,' and to the disciple, 'Here is your mother.' From that time on, this disciple took her into his home" (John 19:26–27). Jesus entrusted the care of his mother to his core friend. This was an honor, not a burden. Let me say this loudly for those of us who struggle with "bothering people": **your needs are not a burden to your core.**

My friend Elizabeth (nickname "E") gets frustrated with me because I don't mention even basic needs she can help meet—like borrowing clothes. I texted her one day bummed about my options for wedding-guest attire, lamenting I had no time to shop. Dumbfounded and a little irritated, she said, "Just get in the car and come see what's in my closet!"

She tells me I don't often expose what I need, and it steals from her the chance to be a better friend. She's right. For the record, it isn't that I *won't* tell her, it's that I don't even think of her as an option. I wasn't taught to see friends as a necessary, designed way that God provides for my needs. I learned either to meet my needs on my own or to diminish them and simply do without—but definitely not to be a "burden" to someone. I will say it again: your needs are not a burden to your core.

If you have a friend like me, please tutor us. Gently remind us that God designed our core relationship to work this way. Coax us into believing it by making *your own* requests for our help. I am delighted to help meet the needs of my core people, and that is what has slowly convinced me they likely feel the same about me. Depth, health, and gratitude of core connection grow deeper and stronger in the grace of meeting one another's needs. Core people delight in the offering. Just like the love of God, the love of a core teaches us to receive grace, which is always undeserved. It primes us to receive the ultimate grace from God in the deepest place of human need: forgiveness from our sin. Your core will make it more possible for you to believe that God generously, freely served you when he didn't need to. You have a Father who met your need in Jesus by his grace: "God demonstrates his own love for us in this: While we were still sinners, Christ died for us" (Rom. 5:8).

The outcome of building a core is intimacy. Intimacy is a comfort level with these special few that is not shared with anyone else. It allows for a unique subset of experiences that you can imagine only having with these specific few. For me, one of those is travel. I see that Jesus retreated, rested, and traveled a lot with his core. When I have tried to travel with friends or family, I am always the most relaxed with my core. Unsurprisingly, when my husband and I have traveled with our core, we notice a similar vibe that makes trips easier: we have the same notion of rest versus activity, similar priorities about how to spend money, and agree on the same number of days we are comfortable leaving our kids. It just kind of *works*.

I've only had one migraine in my entire life, and it was at the end of a trip with a few people I thought were in my core who actually shouldn't have been. The travel brought out our utter lack of alignment, and it has remained the worst trip I've ever taken. I spent the week constantly trying to manage different feelings and logistics and expectations— not fun. Building your core might be a chicken-or-egg scenario: Do you become friends with your core because of like-mindedness? Or do you grow together over time, influencing and serving and loving one another in ways that create synchronicity? The forming of a core is hard to explain: it's definitely grace plus time plus some X factors. However, one thing you *always* have to do to develop a core is *consciously choose to invest in them*.

Choosing Your Core

If you consider all the relationships you wrote down at the end of chapter 1, which two or three names would make up your core? For some people it's hard to choose. My daughter is like that: she has a welcoming, open nature of the most extreme kind. It reminds me of a woman who tried to convince me she had fourteen people in her core. (No. You don't.) She meets new best friends all the time and often makes friends out of strangers or those others reject. I have tried to coach her on not offering such full, intimate access to her heart when she first meets someone, but she regularly tries to convince me I'm wrong. She just wants them all! I love her welcoming heart, but I've also seen her struggle to connect to a special few. **When you choose everyone, you end up choosing no one.** You really aren't designed with enough capacity for fourteen people to uniquely know you. The time constraint alone is enough to make that impossible, and chances are good that you'll end up with some who don't belong there. *Deciding* who you are highly committed to is a powerful statement to people. It is your choice, but you do need to choose *just a few* in order to fully receive the benefit of a core.

Jesus wasn't born into his core. At some point, he *chose* them. We don't know precisely when these relationships began in Jesus's life, but it was likely he had known Peter, James, and John for years before he called them to come and follow him as disciples. It is rare to have someone appear in your core overnight. While there's no mention of these men in his early childhood years, at some point they began to build closer connection. A decision point came to focus on these three even above his own family during his ministry years.

Sometimes I wonder if that was weird in a culture where family was the center of all things. I know it is still difficult today in some family cultures for people to shift from the core into which they were born to a core they *choose*. Jesus, like us, was born into his first core, which would have included some combination of those surrounding his household: parents, siblings, neighbors, aunts, uncles, cousins, and grandparents. There were likely a few he was very close to as he grew up, but when he was ready to fully pursue the mission of God in his life in a greater way, Jesus announced a redefinition of his core. Because Jewish culture was centered on the family structure and survival depended upon it, Jesus's ruthless focus on his disciples—especially his core— must have created some readjustments of expectations in his family.

I grew up in the Midwest, so I know many families who expect a modern version of the same kind of loyalty and involvement. There's absolutely nothing wrong (and lots of things right) with family in or as your core: you just need to define them, making a choice of the few people who will encourage you to go where God wants to take you. There is great richness if you can have family in this part of your relational world. That hasn't been my story, and there's a part of me that feels like I did something wrong because my family of origin is not in my core. However, Jesus had no such hang-up, based on his words in Mark 3 when his family came to "take charge of him" thinking he was "out of his mind" (v. 21). They arrived as Jesus was teaching a big crowd. He was actively engaged in what God had called him to do in his life, and they tried to drag him out of it. They presumptively tried to operate in the primary position in his life based on some combination of the past, duty, or tradition.

> Then Jesus' mother and brothers arrived. Standing outside, they sent someone in to call him. A crowd was sitting around him, and they told him, "Your mother and brothers are outside looking for you."
>
> "Who are my mother and my brothers?" he asked.
>
> Then he looked at those seated in a circle around him and said, "Here are my mother and my brothers! Whoever

does God's will is my brother and sister and mother." (Mark 3:31–35)

With these words, Jesus crushed the cultural assumption that your core was always the family with whom you share biology or position. Matthew captured some even tougher words from Jesus that challenged the family-above-all standard: "Anyone who loves their father or mother more than me is not worthy of me; anyone who loves their son or daughter more than me is not worthy of me. . . . Whoever finds their life will lose it, and whoever loses their life for my sake will find it" (Matt. 10:37, 39).

The people who encourage you to know Jesus and go where he is leading you are the people who belong in your core. You may need a redefinition of the boundaries around your core. If your intent in doing so is to value and follow Jesus the most, go confidently, knowing any sense of loss for his sake will lead to new life. I understand the tugs on your heart and the voice in your head saying it can't be right to do that. Family is a beautiful gift. But Jesus is better.

> **The people who encourage you to know Jesus and go where he is leading you are the people who belong in your core.**

The relationships with my family of origin are not in the core of my life. We don't have the same mission. We cannot share the necessary intimacy, fully and openly communicating. We don't rest or travel well together. Most of us could never pray together. All these things found in a great core are missing. I could probably spend a lot of time in therapy exploring why that is the state of things, but the current truth, whether

I like it or not, is that my family of origin isn't among the two or three people in the world best suited for the kind of relationship Jesus had with Peter, James, and John. By all means let's pursue love and reconciliation to mend or grow these important family connections, but please don't make the mistake of offering people the privileges and access of being a core relationship if they do not support the essence of this space, which is to deeply know you, love you unconditionally, and encourage your pursuit of God's purposes for your life.

Core Loneliness

Your core should play the role of the "last one standing" with you in any situation—especially when you're in trouble. Jesus took his core three with him when he faced the worst and lowest moment of his life. It happened on the night he knew his life was almost over, in the hour in the garden of Gethsemane when he was "overwhelmed with sorrow" (Matt. 26:38). He exposed his deep anguish and asked for their support to watch and to pray for him. When your friends are in pain, this is your chance to step in and be what only the core can be. This is one of the times you do whatever it takes to show up for someone in this space (and where you can consider drawing lines for people who aren't). All Jesus asked from his core when he faced trouble was *presence* and *prayer*. "He took Peter and the two sons of Zebedee along with him, and he began to be sorrowful and troubled. Then he said to them, 'My soul is overwhelmed with sorrow to the point of death. Stay here and keep watch with me. . . . Watch and pray'" (Matt. 26:37–38, 41).

Presence and prayer don't seem like much, but they are everything. I saw the necessity of and my capacity for both of these things when one of my core friends went through a divorce. It was exhausting for her to catch people up on all the ins and outs of what was taking place with her husband, her counselor, her kids, their teachers, and eventually the attorneys and courts. So, even when other friends would check in every week or two, I worked very hard to stay fully present. When your friend is in pain or in crisis, this is no small task. It's something only a core person would undertake. It relieved her so much to have at least one person who kept in step with every little thing because she didn't have the energy to go back and explain. My job was to be present and *stay* present as she walked through the worst.

Because of all the knowledge that afforded me, I had a unique position in prayer. I knew exactly when and how and what to pray. It is the job of a core person to cover you in prayer. I'd pray when we hung up the phone, pray on a text to her in the early morning, set my alarm to pray when she was in court, and pray for her kids' specific struggles. It was constant prayer. When you are in the core, you are the earthly presence of a God who is there in the darkest hour, who will never leave or forsake your friend, like Psalm 23:4 says: "Even though I walk through the darkest valley, I will fear no evil, for you are with me; your rod and your staff, they comfort me."

Jesus understands the pain when your core doesn't come through in that place. It's an experience that makes you feel so very alone. The risk you take as you depend on the people in your core is the risk you're taking in the very worst moments of your life. Not only did Peter, James, and John have trouble staying awake the night Jesus needed them in the garden, but it got even worse. When Jesus was arrested, initially Peter followed as they dragged him away (good move for a core friend!), but by the end of the night he had completely disowned Jesus three different times. It would have hurt for anyone to do it, but your core is supposed to claim you as their own *even in trouble*. This kind of betrayal is especially brutal. Jesus walked into the worst two days of his life knowing that no human was there with him.

I have listened to countless women explain the betrayal or loss of a best friend or a husband who was part of their core. I myself have struggled through the consequences of damage done in these places of trust and intimacy in our early years of marriage when my husband and I were immature and unaware of how precious this space really is. Hurt in this realm of relationship, where the connections are often ten to forty-plus years old, can be life-altering. To lose what was supposed to be unconditional is a wound that only the Lord can heal. But he *can* heal it! Jesus restored his relationship with Peter even after his three denials. The conversation they had to repair this trust has long been the source of my hope that God can help any of us forgive and heal. With Jesus, even complete restoration like Peter experienced is possible.

When Jesus restored his relationship with Peter, he questioned him about his *love*. Three times Jesus asked Peter, "Do you love me?" because *love* is what sets your core people apart (John 21:17). "The third time he said to him, 'Simon son of John, do you love me?' Peter was hurt because Jesus asked him the third time, 'Do you love me?' He said, 'Lord, you know all things; you know that I love you'" (v. 17). Jesus needed Peter to confess and remember that, as part of the core, he was called to unconditional love. He had him repeat it as many times as he'd denied him—a seemingly symbolic way of covering over each denial with grace and reestablishing that connection. Peter went on to be the leader that Jesus called him to be, sharing a close connection to Jesus post-resurrection in the early years of the church, receiving revelation, and laying foundations for the gospel that only the core could be entrusted with.

When a hole gets ripped in your core, it is so understandable to struggle with trust, which can lead to perpetual loneliness in this space. Some of us never forgive. Some of us carry on but never repair or replace that hole. It's a deep kind of loneliness that feels akin to being unloved. Core loneliness is a strong, persistent belief that you are deeply *unknown*. Your core is meant to form a foundation of unconditional love in your life, so when it's missing, there's a unique kind of loneliness that settles in. Sometimes in that hurt or abandoned place you make an agreement with the idea that you are fundamentally unlovable. This is not true! You are worth knowing and you are loved by a God who sacrificed to get you back and wants to be this close to you: "This is how we know what love is: Jesus Christ laid down his life for us" (1 John 3:16). You are worth the life of the only Son of God.

After core pain, my natural reaction is to simply close off the possibility of being hurt again. God has had to remind me—and sometimes prod me—to keep being vulnerable enough to maintain core connections. I often resist this level of exposure, or I find myself retreating into self-protection because of pain I've been through in this space. But Jesus didn't do this. He sought closeness already knowing that his disciples' sin was coming. He knew he couldn't have friendship with these guys without also accepting hurt. We know from Luke 22 that Jesus knew in advance that Peter would deny him: "'But I have prayed for you, Simon, that your faith may not fail. And when you have turned back, strengthen your brothers.' But he replied, 'Lord, I am ready to go with you to prison and to death.' Jesus answered, 'I tell you, Peter, before the rooster crows today, you will deny three times that you know me'" (vv. 32–34).

When you have a strong undercurrent of connection with your Father, you can freely offer trust, love, and connection to others without expecting perfection in return. Actually, without asking for *anything* in return. Unconditional love is the nature of core connection and must be received from the Father, who then equips you to give and receive this love in the lives of others. The only protection and preparation you need for successful core connections is what Jesus had, being "in closest relationship with the Father" (John 1:18).

Psalm 139 is a favorite of mine to read when I hear the lie that I am unknown and unloved at the core of my life. David wrote the words "You have searched me, LORD, and you know me" as a reminder that God knew him better than he knew himself (v. 1). Sometimes I hear the Holy Spirit whisper to me, "Alli, I know you." I've heard these words wash over me in different ways and tones and at so many different times, and it reminds me there is someone who wants to be even closer than a core friend. God has gone out of his way to help me recognize that *he* is most central and the most trusted friend I could have. To remind yourself of the same, whisper this four times out loud—using your own name—with the emphasis on each different word and you'll hear some of what I have heard.

Alli, I know you.

Alli, *I* know you.

Alli, I *know* you.

Alli, I know *you*.

Your Core Is Your Exception

Jesus definitely gave more to his core than to others in his life. And he never apologized for it. If you observe how Jesus interacted in all his relationships, you will quickly see that he did not give even access: some friends had more time and intimacy with him than others did. He went out of his way to make sure that a few had deeper experiences with him, even occasionally *actively preventing* others from coming along to where he took his core, like when he performed the healing of a young girl who was the daughter of a man named Jairus: "He did not let anyone follow him except Peter, James and John" (Mark 5:37). Jesus drew relational boundaries.

If that idea bothers you, then the core might be an uncomfortable space to navigate because these relationships are inherently your *exceptions*. I was an adult before I believed that boundaries are *kind*—to yourself and others. You are a limited person in time and in the emotional capacity required to maintain a deep level of core commitment. Yes, it can occasionally sting when this truth becomes visible in actions. It's hard to be honest about this when feelings are on the line, but if you opt for too many relationships in this space it will reduce the potency of your core. Sensitivity to the feelings of others is a lovely quality; however, over-including will steal strength from this relational space.

My daughter recently captured this struggle when she wasn't invited to the birthday gathering of a friend. I don't care how old you are, that never feels great. In the end she came around and said, "Well, I guess if I only had three people, she wouldn't be one of mine either." I was relieved she was able to see that quickly and manage the emotions of what could have been perceived as a slight. Boundaries are required to give your core the time and space needed to deepen a unique grace from God. But there are many other spaces outside the core that contribute important pieces of a sense of belonging for your soul.

The biggest mistake you could make with your core is not to name them and expressly give them permission to be in this space. So many women have told me that this isn't necessary, saying they each "know how the other feels." This nonverbal mutual understanding isn't going far enough for your core because, to some degree, they are an exception to how your other relationships operate. Unspoken commitment won't unleash the power of the core in your life. If you've never said it out loud, now is the time. Your core needs to be clear on who they are in your life and be given permission to speak and act like others cannot. Tell them they're your exception. Even great friends may hold back out of respect for perceived boundaries without being given the authority to speak into deeper parts of you. Give it to them! These are the people to question you, provide for you, and walk into trouble with you. Accept the mutual responsibility to fully give and receive love in this special part of the ecosystem of your soul. I believe God has buried gold for you inside your core. These people know you. They see you. They're for you. They have wisdom from God for your life and decisions. Tell them you want all of it. Don't let that power, grace, truth, and wisdom from God go untapped!

Who Is Your Core?

Write down the names of anyone who is *definitely* one of your one to three-ish core people here:

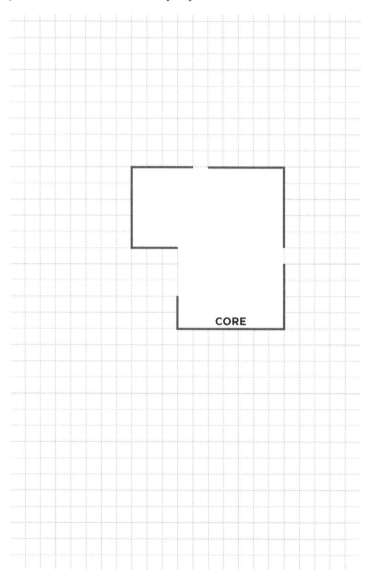

For any name in your core, think about a way you are going to tell them they're your person and give them permission to be completely honest with you. Send it to them right now—email, text, snap, write a letter. Do it however you wish, but set the power of the core loose in your life by telling them.

Write down the names of anyone who *might* be in your core here. Save them for consideration as you read about other parts of the blueprint to come.

Pray this prayer for those people:

Lord, give me either the opportunity to deepen this relationship or the wisdom to see if it isn't for my core. If I am unaware of something, let me see the truth. Help me be brave enough to only welcome into this space people who encourage me to move closer to you. Amen.

If you find yourself with empty boxes above or missing a core relationship that used to be there, take these words from Psalm 90:13–15 and pray them as your own.

Relent, Lord! How long will it be?
    Have compassion on your servants.
Satisfy us in the morning with your unfailing love,
    that we may sing for joy and be glad all our days.
Make us glad for as many days as you have afflicted us,
    for as many years as we have seen trouble.

The core is a special place in the life of your soul to be guarded and treasured, just as Jesus did with Peter, James, and John. Don't be afraid to keep it very small—you weren't designed for many here. The next realm—the **circle**—is a wonderful, rich place of human connection as well.

Live Included by a Circle

The LORD, the LORD, the compassionate and gracious God,
slow to anger, and abounding in loyal love and faithfulness.

Exodus 34:6 NET

One perfect fall evening we were hanging out on our beautiful
screened-in porch with a fire going just outside and a breeze
blowing. My son was playing his guitar. We had drinks and
snacks and some good college football games on our outdoor
TV. It was just about perfect, and I wanted a friend to share
it with. My two best friends (my core) were busy. I was feeling pretty social, so I did something I wouldn't typically do.
I texted someone from work on a whim to come over and
hang out. I know, I know, it doesn't sound like a big deal, but
it was for me. When they didn't respond, I gave up and sat
considering the very short list of people I was willing to text.

I felt a whiff of loneliness on that otherwise perfect evening. I told myself it wasn't real, or if it was, it wasn't valid. After all, I had a great husband right next to me, and my kids actually wanted to be around. My couple of close friends just happened to be unavailable. But I had a nagging feeling it meant a little more than that. That evening had the same vibe as a few other recent instances: there seemed to be regular moments when I felt like a sixteen-year-old with a car on a Friday night but with nowhere to go.

I don't have a well-developed circle.

Those small passing brushes of loneliness were a clue to a significant hole in my relational world. As I look at the blueprint of the life of Jesus, this type of connection is my biggest point of difference. Jesus had twelve guys whom he trained and lived, worked, socialized, and traveled with almost all the time. I, on the other hand, have a couple of people I can go to lunch with if I arrange it at least four weeks in advance, knowing there's at least a 50 percent chance of cancellation. I know another few women who share a work life similar to mine, but they live in other states, so it's Zoom or Voxer or Marco Polo for us. When I compare my own relational world to Jesus's, it's my *circle* that looks severely lacking. This truth also explains my most recent encounters with loneliness—the ones I don't even give myself permission to admit.

The ecosystem of your soul comprises more than just what a core provides: you also need a circle, and they are not the same. Beyond just being good friends, your circle is the crew who repeatedly shows up in your weekly life and is highly connected to your daily activities—job, parenting responsibilities, studies, hobbies—and your weekly places—home, workplace, coffee shop, gym. You share a vibe. They're your day in, day out friends around whom you live the bulk of your life.

For too long I have blamed my weak circle on my current stage of life (raising four active teenagers and working two jobs). I've blown it off as unimportant—especially since I have a core—but lately I've been realizing this is accounting for more loneliness than I want to admit and have been asking God to help me develop this realm of relationship in my life. I really want a few more friends who always invite me and who I can always include in my evening walks or Friday nights. Being included in someone's everyday life is the essence of a true circle. I want more connection with more people who do work like me or who I might see at my eighth weekly stop at the grocery store. I need more friends I can see without a carefully formulated plan on the calendar—and I wouldn't mind a few more people who are definitely going to text me when I wake up tomorrow.

I need a stronger circle.

Building a Circle

Adult friendship is a tricky thing to grow. I want to stay on track with my work, make sure my family is connected and loved well, try to keep my body healthy and my marriage thriving, and at the end of this long list of important things in my days, building friendships seems nearly impossible if it has to be something extra I do outside all those other things. Your circle friendships are the ones *inside* all that stuff. They get built while you're doing whatever you're doing. My circle has atrophied because I have taken the view that these kinds of friendships are either optional, unavailable, or too difficult to pursue. Only in their absence did I finally see they're an essential component of being a whole, healthy soul.

Jesus built a circle with his core three plus nine more men for a total of twelve "best friends." From the very beginning of his circle, the intention was to train them and work and travel together. Before he chose them, he prayed. That sounds like a pretty good idea to me. Whatever he asked his Father, Jesus seemed to receive understanding of who to have near him as he walked daily through his life. God has people in mind for you too!

> Jesus went up on a mountainside and called to him those he wanted, and they came to him. He appointed twelve that they might be with him and that he might send them out to preach and to have authority to drive out demons. These are the twelve he appointed: Simon (to whom he gave the name Peter), James son of Zebedee and his brother John (to them he gave the name Boanerges, which means "sons of thunder"), Andrew, Philip, Bartholomew, Matthew, Thomas, James son of Alphaeus, Thaddaeus, Simon the Zealot and Judas Iscariot, who betrayed him. (Mark 3:13–19)

Twelve isn't an obligatory number, but as you evaluate your own relationships at the end of this chapter, think in numbers close to that. Modern psychological and relational research suggests this rough number is a relational threshold that has relevance for *all* humans. Humans seem designed with a capacity for relationships that doesn't widely vary. Social media has fooled us into thinking we can develop more friendships than we actually have the bandwidth for. You may be fond of someone's approach to family or style or work or humor and follow them on social media, but that does not qualify them for your circle. The threshold for truly intimate human relationships seems to be no more than five (tops for a core), and the total number of better friendships people seem capable of maintaining with regularity is in the ballpark of fifteen (tops for your core plus circle). These thresholds not only validate patterns of relationships in the life of Jesus but also point to an innate, God-given design to your relational world. If you try to operate significantly outside of this, chances are good your inner and outer life will end up the poorer for it.

After Jesus prayed, he initiated contact with these guys: he asked them to come and be with him while they were doing something—teaching, preaching, healing—and these activities were the basis for their daily connection. These friendships were built in Jesus's life while they were busy becoming disciples—learning, practicing, and growing together in the life of the kingdom that Jesus was teaching them. Circles are built when you're thinking about building something other than the relationship. Even though there might be work and activity in common, no one wants to hang out with people they don't genuinely like. These twelve men were also "those he wanted" (Mark 3:13). There must have been a significant element of personal affinity if Jesus *wanted* to be around them.

I like runners. I always seem to have a natural affinity for them no matter their age, gender, ethnicity, etc. Runners show a propensity for disciplined living and positive attitudes. Maybe it's all the endorphins and the love of time outside. Whatever accounts for the connection, I like more runners than I don't. I initially took up running as an easy way to maintain my physical and mental health, but most other long-term runners shared my mission to live a healthy lifestyle in a lot of other ways. Both the *affinity* and the shared *activity* make runners a great starting place for building up my circle. This is a group God has often brought me back to as I've considered how to better build a circle because I'm running most days of the week anyway!

You need something to do *shoulder to shoulder* with your circle—running, knitting, working, riding motorcycles, raising toddlers, camping, reading, volunteering at an animal shelter, or just walking your dog. A circle is built when you do more than talk. If you aren't going anywhere, then no one can come along for the ride. Someone who's doing the same work is a great candidate for your circle. We often make distinctions between our "real friends" and our "work friends," but Jesus made no such distinction. It was common in ancient Jewish culture for men to spend hours and years creating their best friendships while studying and memorizing the Torah together. Jesus trained his friends, and friendship grew as they worked—several pairs of Jesus's disciples were either brothers or business partners or both prior to becoming his disciples. I once became friends with a coworker after the delightful discovery that she rolled her eyes or stifled a laugh at all the same moments I did in a meeting we had together. We made quite a pair! Working and living alongside someone creates the opportunity to discover more and more about each other. Jesus knew this created more than work connections when he sent his own disciples out two by two to do some work together.

> Then Jesus went around teaching from village to village. Calling the Twelve to him, he began to send them out two by two and gave them authority over impure spirits.
>
> These were his instructions: "Take nothing for the journey except a staff—no bread, no bag, no money in your belts. Wear sandals but not an extra shirt. Whenever you enter a house, stay there until you leave that town. And if any place will not welcome you or listen to you, leave that place and shake the dust off your feet as a testimony against them."
>
> They went out and preached that people should repent. They drove out many demons and anointed many sick people with oil and healed them. (Mark 6:6–13)

The pairs of men came back excited at what they'd discovered together. They'd no doubt had to rely upon each other, finding resources, practicing their message, and getting encouragement from each other when they got rejected along the way. Jesus was an amazing leader who certainly knew friendships are deepened as you work. It's possible some of the disciples may not have even liked each other much at first, especially the one who came straight out of a job as a hated tax collector. The condition for growing a circle is wanting something besides a friend. These guys all wanted Jesus, discipleship, and the kingdom of God. It was a great starting place.

I have developed circle friends through sharing a passion for education or the Bible, going to the same gym at the same time, desiring community on the same street, rearing kids the same age, or having common work or a common boss. Geography plays a more important role here than it does for the core since *doing something together* is the access point for the connection. Digital spaces make it possible to share activity and remain physically distant more than ever, but I'm still wrestling with that dynamic. I can feel the missing layer of connection when a screen is between people. So is connection online possible? Yes. Ideal? Perhaps not.

Choosing a Circle

Truth be told, though, you can survive without a circle. I'm proof of it. Circle friends are not essential for *surviving*, but they are essential for *thriving*. You can make it without a strong circle. I've been doing it, but I'm tired of being in survival mode. I want to live a life I love, and making the choice to cultivate a circle is key to that. I'll always need to do laundry and get my job done and show up at my kids' concerts, but if I can sit by a friend when I get there, maybe the places I go would feel more deeply meaningful to my soul. Because you can do without it, circle friendship is only built when it is freely chosen. Jesus explicitly told his disciples, "I chose you" (John 15:16), and he called them friends. These were the twelve men who were always invited, always included, and always present with Jesus, day after day.

Jesus didn't let just anyone into his circle. He chose his twelve not just for their work but also for their heart underneath it. Occasionally someone else would ask to follow Jesus in as close a proximity as the Twelve were. Jesus always pushed back, wanting to know if they were like-minded, prepared to grow, and ready to invest even if there was a significant cost. Jesus was about growing the kingdom and character of God in his followers. Anyone hoping to come in closer was challenged: Did they see God was doing something in him? Did they move according to his values? He wanted alignment of hearts as much as activities.

> As they were walking along the road, a man said to him, "I will follow you wherever you go." Jesus replied, "Foxes have dens and birds have nests, but the Son of Man has no place to lay his head."
>
> He said to another man, "Follow me." But he replied, "Lord, first let me go and bury my father." Jesus said to him, "Let the dead bury their own dead, but you go and proclaim the kingdom of God."
>
> Still another said, "I will follow you, Lord; but first let me go back and say goodbye to my family." Jesus replied, "No one who puts a hand to the plow and looks back is fit for service in the kingdom of God." (Luke 9:57–62)

I made a mom friend with kids similar ages to mine. She was tons of fun to be with and often available to meet up at our local spots. We had easy access, good affinity, and common work as moms. But she lied to her kids. For real. She wouldn't have said it like that, but she lied to them *all the time*. It bothered me deep in my heart. It was just the way she operated if she didn't want to deal with difficult things or explain something sad or try to communicate an adult idea on their level. She just made up a story, an excuse, or a fake version of reality for everything from the death of a loved one to how Jesus and Santa teamed up to pull off Christmas. Whatever worked for her in the moment is what she said.

I, on the other hand, try to talk to my kids in super honest, straightforward ways—probably to a fault. No one is leaving my house uninformed: I like the hard facts. To me, this is a critical part of building trust and respect between us. My girls still laugh about the time I pulled over on the side of the road and googled a chart of the female reproductive system to answer a question one of them asked. It's possible I'm a little bit over the top. My friend and I shared the external work of motherhood, but our internal convictions about how to do that were almost hilariously far apart. We had unresolvable conflict a couple times over my refusal to corroborate some of her stories. It didn't work for us to be in the same circle because the convictions in our hearts around parenting styles were just too different. Neither of us were looking for a change of heart. Could we be friends? Yes. In the same circle? Not for long.

Choosing a circle doesn't mean choosing people who always think or act the same as you—please don't do that! I had someone in my circle for many years who thought nearly the opposite of any political opinion I ever had. We did share, however, a value on trying to follow Jesus and a belief that friendship is a great place for passionate, deep, intelligent sharpening. Trouble comes in your circle when a misalignment of your nonnegotiables causes you to pursue life in continuing opposite directions. A circle is about *pursuing the mission of your life together* and encouraging one another as you go. If you're a half step off from someone else in your circle, ask yourself why. Is it something you can sharpen, encourage, and challenge in one another? Or is it an essential difference that will always pull you apart? There are other realms of relationship; acknowledging you need an adjustment might preserve what's good about the connection.

Your circle, similar to your core, also must be made up of people to whom you are willing to show your authentic self. Jesus showed his twelve more of who he was than he showed his community or the crowds he regularly taught. Although all twelve disciples didn't get the same intimate experiences as Peter, James, and John did, they did receive many more layers of his heavenly insight than most people: "His disciples asked him what this parable meant. He said, 'The knowledge of the secrets of the kingdom of God has been given to you, but to others I speak in parables'" (Luke 8:9–10). Jesus also allowed his circle to see his divine power, like when he commanded nature itself in Matthew 8:27: "The men were amazed and asked, 'What kind of man is this? Even the winds and the waves obey him!'" Circles share, so the trust between you should create openness and authenticity to share parts of yourself you wouldn't expose to just anyone, like Jesus did in his relationship with his Father:

> One day Jesus was praying in a certain place. When he finished, one of his disciples said to him, "Lord, teach us to pray, just as John taught his disciples."

He said to them, "When you pray, say:

> "'Father, hallowed be your name,
>   your kingdom come.
> Give us each day our daily bread.
> Forgive us our sins,
>   for we also forgive everyone who sins against us.
> And lead us not into temptation.'" (Luke 11:1–4)

They asked, and Jesus showed them. That's the open nature of a circle. The disciples often questioned Jesus, even to the point of challenge. They externally processed with him without the need to be buttoned up. They asked special favors from him for their own family, like when Jesus healed Simon's mother-in-law: "Now Simon's mother-in-law was suffering from a high fever, and they asked Jesus to help her" (Luke 4:38). And Jesus showed the same trust and confidence in them. He told them things ahead of other people, even allowing them to know the details of his own death ahead of time:

> Now Jesus was going up to Jerusalem. On the way, he took the Twelve aside and said to them, "We are going up to Jerusalem, and the Son of Man will be delivered over to the chief priests and the teachers of the law. They will condemn him to death and will hand him over to the Gentiles to be mocked and flogged and crucified. On the third day he will be raised to life!" (Matt. 20:17–19)

Jesus gave his guys information and asked them not to tell anyone. The ability to talk with honesty, openness, and confidence has always been the earmark of closer friendships. Writings from Jewish rabbis at the time of Jesus hail this friendship quality, as well as Proverbs like these:

An honest answer
is like a kiss on the lips. (Prov. 24:26)

A gossip betrays a confidence;
so avoid anyone who talks too much. (Prov. 20:19)

I told my teenagers if they can respect the confidences of their circles, they will avoid the vast majority of drama in middle school and high school. Come to think of it, maybe you can avoid a good amount of it for your whole life if you can control your tongue! Good circles don't break confidences no matter what incentive they're given. Friends keep their mouths shut.

Well, except at dinner—the hallmark of a circle is opening your mouth and eating together. After work, you have drinks. After a run, you grab coffee. After class, you hit the dining hall. Growth and joy in these friendships mix beautifully with sitting around a table. Jesus's twelve ate together from the very beginning of their story to the very end. When Jesus called Levi, the tax collector, into his circle, he ate with him. Among Jewish people, meals were a serious point of cultural connection and belonging with fellow Jews. You only ate with those who hit the legal marks of cleanliness and adhered to the Jewish dietary laws. When Jesus ate with Levi, it was scandalous because he was offering the central gesture of religious, personal, and cultural acceptance to someone who others found unacceptable. This is the kind of acceptance you have with Jesus too. He has made room in his circle for you, welcoming you despite all the objections of others, your messy past, or your questionable ethics and morals.

Then Levi held a great banquet for Jesus at his house, and a large crowd of tax collectors and others were eating with them. But the Pharisees and the teachers of the law who belonged to their sect complained to his disciples, "Why do you eat and drink with tax collectors and sinners?"

Jesus answered them, "It is not the healthy who need a doctor, but the sick. I have not come to call the righteous, but sinners to repentance." (Luke 5:29–32)

I once hosted an "I like you" dinner for about ten women from work. That's exactly what I said when I invited them: "I just like you and I want to have dinner together." I assigned everyone an element to bring for a salad bar, from croutons to salmon, and hosted in my own dining room. There were women there from assistants to members of the leadership team. Our commonalities were Jesus, work, and salads—and my fondness for the women around the table. I didn't have the language of *circle* at the time, but this was clearly a personal attempt to build a better one. The meal was my gesture of connection and my request for more intimacy and friendship. All of that grows well over dinner with wine and lingering conversations.

Jesus feels this way about you. You're invited to his table to grow in circle-like friendship. Bring yourself to him, relaxed and open, to receive his gesture of real friendship. For me this looks exactly like it does over dinner with friends: I speak honestly, I'm open to their words, and I try to hear ways I can serve and love them in daily life.

The final act of friendship between Jesus and his twelve disciples was also a meal, called the Last Supper. This is where he made it clear they had become "forever friends" (even though that sounds a tad cheesy, calling them his "ride or die" doesn't seem right for this occasion). Jesus said the deepest act of a circle is to include them in his life forever, and he was going to the cross to make it possible.

> My command is this: Love each other as I have loved you. Greater love has no one than this: to lay down one's life for one's friends. You are my friends if you do what I command. I no longer call you servants, because a servant does not know his master's business. Instead, I have called you friends, for everything that I learned from my Father I have made known to you. (John 15:12–15)

Loving your circle well looks like obsessive inclusion, even to the point of sacrifice. You can love your circle by inviting and including them without exception—even when others object or want to exclude them. Circles exist to be the faithful, steadfast presence of a God whose compassion and grace for you simply don't end.

Who invites you and includes you all the time? Who do you do that for? Jesus included these disciples in his circle by sharing everything he had to offer, right down to his very life. Though he was God, he didn't want any separation between them based on position or past or power. "Instead, I have called you friends" (v. 15). Jesus purposely leveled the playing field that night, taking the position of a servant to wash their feet. Any distinctions of wealth or class—anything that puts you above or below someone—is not something that should separate friends in a circle. It's ultimately a tool to be used to bless and share with your circle all that you have.

For a few years I had a small circle of women who were amazing at doing this. Each of us—a CEO of a restaurant group, a stylist, an EVP of a large company, and me, a teacher and author—had a significant resource or gift at our disposal. It seemed like each time we met, someone was serving all the others, sending encouraging words, planning a prayer retreat, paying the check, or giving haircuts, small gifts, free books, a special bottle of wine, a timely reservation, or the use of someone's office space for an event. This particular group of women had a strong instinct for using whatever resource they had and turning it into a blessing for everyone else. This is the motivation of great circles.

Loneliness in a Circle

Sometimes people in my circle have just disappeared. That group is a great example. For a couple years we were all about inclusion and invitation. But now, several years later, the connections have shifted. I'd still sit down and have a great chat with any of them today, but it's not the same dynamic: only one person has stayed in my circle. Jesus's circle was stable for the three years of his public ministry and the training of those twelve men. And then circumstances changed. Before those years, it isn't clear precisely what all the guys' connections were like. Some of them certainly knew each other. For three years, however, they were a very tight circle.

You might find your circle shifts every few years as well. Sometimes that's painful. In my life it's definitely been the cause of hurt and loneliness, even when I've understood exactly why they've drifted or shifted. Circles can be wonderfully close and invested, but in the life of Jesus they weren't permanent. I tend to like deeper and long-lasting relationships (hence why I have a strong core but not a great circle), but I believe the semi-changing nature of circles gives you the opportunity to shift and change as your life circumstances and your soul needs do. Remember, a circle isn't about how much you like someone, it's about affinity *and* activity—who you need in your life in that season.

But it still hurts when someone leaves. Or when you receive a long-standing tear in this part of your soul from the betrayal of a close friend, which Jesus also experienced.

> **Remember, a circle isn't about how much you like someone, it's about affinity *and* activity—who you need in your life in that season.**

The height of circle betrayal in Jesus's life was from his friend and disciple Judas Iscariot. Judas sold Jesus out for money. He put a price tag on Jesus's worth to him, even after they'd sat at countless tables, traveled countless miles, and said countless prayers. Jesus and Judas relaxed together in a tight circle of belonging every day for years. When the connection was torn, the ripple effect on both their lives meant nothing was ever the same again. If you've been betrayed by someone in your circle, you understand how he felt.

Anything remotely like that kind of betrayal—or even the threat of it—can set loose the whispers of loneliness that echo in this part of your soul, telling you, "I guess you never really belonged" or "No one's even thinking about you." Circle loneliness says you don't belong together anymore—and maybe you never did. You're outside the circle, and "No one even cares if you're there or not." These words of loneliness hurt deeply, especially if you once felt a strong sense of belonging together. The voice of rejection may be quick to speak about your circle because the power of a circle lies in the fact that you are *always included*. Those kinds of words from the voice of rejection bounding around your mind and heart make it hard to believe you'll ever feel like you belong again. But you will! God wants to rebuild my circle and yours. He wants to invite you first into a deeper sense of belonging with him and then into a new season with others here on earth who will express his faithfulness to you again. You belong with him, and there's a place of belonging he already sees for you with others.

Paul, an apostle Jesus called into his circle post-resurrection, recognized that the behavior of an inner circle is to personify godly support and belonging. He was ashamed of his own past and didn't think he deserved to be included in Jesus's circle after rejecting Jesus and violently persecuting his followers. It was true: Paul violated everything a circle is supposed to do. Paul said in 1 Corinthians 15:3–9, "It was fitting that I bring up the rear. I don't deserve to be included in that inner circle, as you well know, having spent all those early years trying my best to stamp God's church right out of existence" (MSG).

But Jesus invited Paul anyway, and it restored his soul and transformed him into a godly man and friend. Jesus told him he was still worthy, welcome, invited, and included—just as you are. By the time he wrote those words, Paul had discovered that being connected to Jesus was a huge key in helping him connect with others. Being received into the inner circle of God gave him a permanent place to belong, a lasting sense of being included. Paul soon walked and worked with a sense of his own value and the confidence that he was gifted by God himself— things only knowing Jesus can help you receive. Being a friend of Jesus fills you up with the worth of being willingly chosen, always included, and consistently invited into a life you don't deserve. This kind of love will bring life to your very soul. The circle of friends you keep in your life are there to demonstrate a flesh and blood experience of the gracious, undeserved, absolutely faithful love of belonging to Jesus.

God **picked you out as his** from the very start. Think of it: **included** in God's original plan of salvation by the bond of faith in the living truth. This is the life of the Spirit **he invited you to** through the Message we delivered, in which you get in on the glory of our Master, Jesus Christ. (2 Thess. 2:13–14 MSG, emphasis added)

Your Circle Is Your Future

As soon as I met the college housemates of our Gracie, I saw the power a circle had to change you, little by little. Gracie was our family's longtime favorite babysitter. She not only worked for us in the summers but had traveled with us and shared life with us for many years. She was part of the family, so one fall we visited her in college. We knocked on the door of her house and heard her sweet voice floating back through the open window, saying, "Oh my gosh, they're here!" When the door flung open, I realized the voice actually belonged to her best friend, Kate. The inflection, the cadence, the tone of her words sounded exactly like Gracie! Then we met Leslie and heard Gracie's lighthearted sarcasm and felt her same down-to-earth vibe. Then we talked with Emily and laughed at her quoting the same song lyrics Gracie did and sprinkling the same phrases and slang words throughout their conversation. A few years of living together day in, day out had enhanced their likeness both internally and externally. They shared tones and gestures but also perspectives and ethics. Sure, some similarities may have existed pre-friendship, explaining the initial spark, but there was no doubt that intense togetherness had caused a unifying evolution of heart, mind, and character.

That's the power of a circle. Jesus knew this would happen, too, which is why he spent three years living and working with his own twelve guys in a tight circle. It was the best way for the character, words, and priorities of his Father's kingdom to work their way from the outside to the inside of these men for a lifetime.

Your circle isn't neutral. Its impact on your life is immeasurable. When I was a preteen, my mom said, "Choose your friends wisely: you'll become who they are." It sounded weak-minded to me, as if my character could be blown around by any random person. Turns out, she wasn't far off. (Moms usually aren't.) There's a real thing called the social proximity effect. Because God designed us to be impacted by relationships, we do, in fact, absorb both positive and negative things from the people around us. We pick up gestures, health choices, spending habits, and all kinds of other things from people in our regular proximity. The circle has power simply because they're the ones you're with!

Of course, you can make your own decisions, and you have your own mind and values, but the circle exerts power like a small, frequent tide slowly pulling you in a direction that is largely imperceptible on any given day and, therefore, very difficult to resist. The habits, attitudes, and character of your circle will have an impact on your behaviors. It's those daily actions that create your future, for better and for worse. Paul shared the truth of this in his warning to the Corinthian church through the words of Greek poet Menander: "Bad company corrupts good character" (1 Cor. 15:33), and the book of Proverbs recognizes the same wisdom throughout, capturing it succinctly in Proverbs 13:20:

> Walk with the wise and become wise,
>   for a companion of fools suffers harm.

Who Is Your Circle?

You can tell a lot about your relationship with someone by how they treat you and talk about you when you're not around. Your circle would defend any misrepresentation of your name or character, and they certainly wouldn't give you up to your enemies. But the night Jesus was in the garden of Gethsemane, one in his circle did just that. In a stunning betrayal of his friend and teacher, Judas Iscariot showed up with soldiers to arrest Jesus. The others in the circle were shocked. "When Jesus' followers saw what was going to happen, they said, 'Lord, should we strike with our swords?' And one of them struck the servant of the high priest, cutting off his right ear" (Luke 22:49–50).

If you've ever had a friend like this, my guess is you don't mind that their love for you is a little unhinged. I had a friend in my circle for a handful of years who was the cut-off-someone's-ear type. I once described some particularly harsh criticism I received in response to a sermon I gave, and her response was, "I'm gonna find out where they live." Maybe it was her southern Mississippi combination of camo-and-shotguns plus seersucker-and-monograms, but I'd never had a friend before who would so readily defend me and do it with a smile on her face. I didn't mind that an ear ended up on the ground every now and then, and she wasn't a bit sorry for it. If you're happy you've got someone in your corner like this, write their name in the box at the end of this chapter.

Before you write more names, a few words of caution: don't just write down the ten to fifteen people you *like* the most. Affinity is critical in the circle, but it's not enough. There is a woman I adore whose name I cannot legitimately write in my circle, as much as its pains me not to. We have plenty of affection for each other, and I love every moment I get to see her. However, we have *zero* access to each other's lives. You need access to these people in the regular rhythm of life. She lives forty-five minutes from me, and we have eight kids between us, so shared time is rare. There's simply no opportunity for regular activity together. **Access** and **activity** are just as important as **affinity** in this realm of relationship.

And listen up, parents! This is the part of your relational world where you may need to account for your children. The time and energy you put into children—especially those at home from the ages of five to around twenty—require a circle-type daily attention and activity. The needs of infants and little ones require even more special consideration, and this is a rare season when much of your relational capacity is engaged in their care. Give yourself lots of grace and maybe count them as double in this realm for the first few years. The impact of children on your relational world is huge and must be considered as you think about your heart and capacity to pursue all the realms of relationships you need.

Some of you may have adult children who have shifted into a true core connection, or maybe you're now out of daily or weekly contact, so they feel more like comrades or community. Just think specifically about each child as you consider the full picture of your relational world, because actively raising children with loving care means they take up space in you, a relational soul. And they should! I have four teenage children, and this space seems best for how I want to connect and love them in this phase of life. They have a significant impact on my capacity to pursue other relationships. Things shift as they grow, so don't be afraid to rethink it later. Remember, circles shift every few years.

Consider the following questions and write in this part of your blueprint the names of the five to ten people who are truly in your circle:

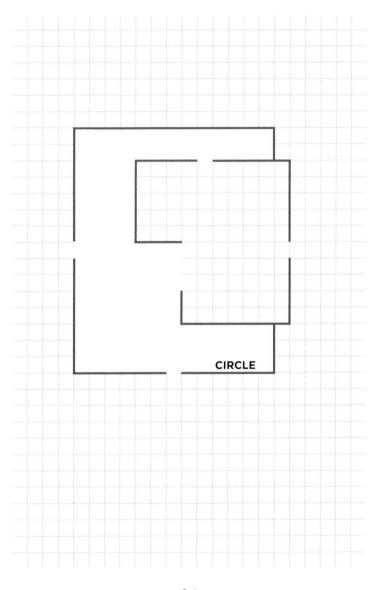

CIRCLE

- Who is mentored or invested in by you regularly (including your kids)?
- Who would you invite over for drinks on a Friday night in your sweats?
- Whose gatherings do you always know you'll be invited to?
- Who do you look to sit with in classes or staff meetings?
- Who has something good in their life you'd like to have in yours in two to three years?
- Who do you do sports/activities/hobbies with?
- Who brags about you or recommends you to other people?
- Who didn't run away the last time you were in trouble or were a mess?
- Who do you eat with regularly?
- Who have you traveled with outside of your immediate family?

Who *might* be in your circle? Use this box to write names of people you thought might be in your circle but could actually be in another realm. Put a pin in these until you read on.

Now, read Psalm 1 and pray this prayer:

Blessed is the one
　　who does not walk in step with the wicked
or stand in the way that sinners take
　　or sit in the company of mockers,
but whose delight is in the law of the LORD,
　　and who meditates on his law day and night.
That person is like a tree planted by streams of
　　water,
　　which yields its fruit in season
and whose leaf does not wither—
　　whatever they do prospers.

Not so the wicked!
　　They are like chaff
　　that the wind blows away.
Therefore the wicked will not stand in the judgment,
　　nor sinners in the assembly of the righteous.
For the LORD watches over the way of the righteous,
　　but the way of the wicked leads to destruction.

Father, help me to see who you've brought into my life to enjoy in my days and weeks and to help shape and encourage me to be the person you made me to be. Help me wisely choose friends who delight in you and are trying to grow. Direct my steps away from anyone I've brought in close who shouldn't be there, and help me recognize that their influence needs to stop. Watch over my path and give me good discernment on all the relationships around me. Amen.

Live Encouraged by Comrades

Fight the good fight of the faith. Take hold of the eternal life to which you were called when you made your good confession in the presence of many witnesses.

1 Timothy 6:12

I walked into a room on a campus in Nashville, Tennessee, wondering for a moment if I was in the right place. The faces staring back at me didn't look anything like mine, so I immediately questioned the room number on my document. There was a group of younger people who looked closer to my kids' ages than my own and a few men who were at least twenty years my senior, two of whom were standing in a corner together speaking Spanish. I knew no one else in the room was a wife and mother of four small kids. However, after multiple long days together, I cried as I drove away from them and out of Nashville.

I'd never been in a room full of people at the same point in their training for exactly the same mission I was on. Gender and age and ethnicity faded to the background because every person in the room wanted as much as I did to learn and teach the Word of God. I'd been in seminary as a distance student, so I worked alone almost all the time. What I felt in the room was the presence and power of **comrades**—people on a specific kind of mission, working to grow a similar kind of fruit. In our hearts we had the same desires, the same questions, the same goals. In John 15, Jesus called his disciples "branches" growing off the same vine, tended by the same gardener (v. 5). In that room we were **comrades** doing the same physical work on the same spiritual mission. I'd never felt it before.

When I think of the word *comrade* I think of the military. I've never served in the armed forces, but I know the old expression *comrade in arms* refers to fellow soldiers. The true essence of the phrase indicates something even more specific: it's a fellow soldier who faced the same enemy and stood with you in the same battle. You need comrades. You need a layer of people in your relational world working on the same mission, helping you face your assignment and equipping you for the battles that inevitably follow. Comrades are your resources, strength, and encouragement from God for the work you do every day. For Christians, kingdom comrades like I found in that room in Nashville are essential for spiritual thriving.

Whether or not you're a Christian, God created you to physically perform meaningful work on the earth. To the very first man and woman God said, "Be fruitful and increase in number; fill the earth and subdue it. Rule over the fish in the sea and the birds in the sky and over every living creature that moves on the ground" (Gen. 1:28). Every human being has a physical nature that was created to desire satisfying work. God designed humanity to find and increase the potential of his good creation and bring order to it with leadership that honors him. Your whole soul was created *with this assignment in mind*. This means your soul was made with a need for relationships that encourage you to fulfill your part of this charge to humanity. In this season of your life, maybe you need comrades on the battlefield of parenting children in our culture today. You may need some who can help you run a business or serve in public office with godly leadership. You may need a medical community who sees bodies and healing through eyes of faith, or others who want to protect green space or parks in the city where you live. Whatever part you play right now in God's command from Genesis 1:28, you're made to share the mission of your life with others.

Beyond your physical labors, you need comrades because you are part of a spiritual battle. Everyone who comes into the family of Christ joins an ongoing fight for human souls. You receive gifts and opportunities to work alongside God in the rescue mission spoken of in Colossians 1:13 to bring people into the kingdom of God: "For he has rescued us from the dominion of darkness and brought us into the kingdom of the Son he loves." Even if you've never considered yourself a part of a kingdom on a mission, you have one! The church are your comrades in arms for this battle. You were made to take part in the Great Commission that Jesus gave his followers before departing from earth. These words indicate a collective mission for comrades in arms. "Jesus came to them and said, 'All authority in heaven and on earth has been given to me. Therefore go and make disciples of all nations, baptizing them in the name of the Father and of the Son and of the Holy Spirit, and teaching them to obey everything I have commanded you'" (Matt. 28:18–20). When you are born physically *and* spiritually, your inner being is created with these work assignments in mind. Cultivating relationships with fellow soldiers is critical to a fulfilling, fruitful, victorious life and to maintaining a healthy soul. You need encouragement from other people to take part in the mission of God here on earth.

My cousin is one of my comrades. We live five states and 940 miles apart, so she really can't function as part of my circle (but man, I wish she could). Nonetheless, God gave us an X factor–connection of heart and mission. Sure, our shared community of extended family made it easier to find each other, but it goes way beyond familial connection. We discovered commonalities in the way we live, the mission of our home and family, the use of our money, a shared passion for education, and a love for learning and teaching Scripture. The basis of our connection isn't just family: it's that we are comrades on the same mission. We can encourage each other. We grow in understanding of the Bible together and sharpen each other. We can pray and fast together. Even five states apart, we are connected because of mission.

This was the same for Jesus and his cousin John the Baptist. They, too, were in the same family but were comrades with connected assignments from God. John explained, "'I am not the Messiah but am sent ahead of him.' The bride belongs to the bridegroom. The friend who attends the bridegroom waits and listens for him, and is full of joy when he hears the bridegroom's voice. That joy is mine, and it is now complete. He must become greater; I must become less" (John 3:28–30). John came as a witness to testify before Jesus, to prepare others for Jesus and Jesus for others, even baptizing him as his public ministry began. John wasn't directly in his circle during the era we have recorded in the Bible, but their shared trajectory, vision, and heart made them highly connected comrades.

The comrades in your life probably have a lot in common with your circle. Comrades often share aligned hearts and missions but *mis*aligned circumstances like geography, schedules, opportunities, or social or cultural barriers. In the life of Jesus, his closest comrades appear to be the sibling trio of Mary, Martha, and Lazarus. Their deep conviction that Jesus was the Messiah (John 11:27) gave them the same heart and mission as his twelve disciples, but cultural and geographic circumstances made them comrades instead. The sisters first provided resources and hospitality to Jesus as he traveled through their village—this was a culturally acceptable way for women to interact with Jesus. Mary pushed in even closer while he was in their home, taking the posture of a true disciple. Jesus allowed her to receive from him as such: "As Jesus and his disciples were on their way, he came to a village where a woman named Martha opened her home to him. She had a sister called Mary, who sat at the Lord's feet listening to what he said" (Luke 10:38–39).

His time there (and likely other similar visits) formed a deeper friendship, and they fell into the thicker gray area between circle and comrades. This strong connection was put on display when Lazarus became very sick and the sisters asked Jesus to come help "the one you love" (John 11:3). When he arrived, Lazarus had died. The depth of their connection was on display as Jesus wept over the death of his friend. Then Lazarus was the recipient of Jesus's most astounding miracle: Jesus raised him back to life after four days in the grave! Comrades can be deep, highly consequential relationships in your life.

The realm of comrades in Jesus's life ranged from heart-level friendships with Mary, Martha, and Lazarus to a larger group of coworkers who were committed to his mission, simply known in Scripture as "the seventy-two." Jesus equipped this larger army of disciples for his kingdom work, and they were part of his mission to spread the gospel.

> After this the Lord appointed seventy-two others and sent them two by two ahead of him to every town and place where he was about to go. He told them, "The harvest is plentiful, but the workers are few. Ask the Lord of the harvest, therefore, to send out workers into his harvest field." (Luke 10:1–2)

The mission and the work of Jesus's ministry connected these comrades. Though some no doubt shared a more personal connection to Jesus, the foundation of all his comrade relationships was their shared commitment to spread the message of the kingdom of God. Any intimacy created in this realm of relationship happens through the battles on the battlefield. Just before Jesus sent the seventy-two out to practice sharing the good news together, he talked about the cost of following him: theirs was a mission that demanded a willingness to give up anything—even tradition, family, and home. Comrades of all kinds have counted the same costs you have; they're "in" at the same level. You need life-giving encouragement from people facing the same battles. Comrades are the ones you trust for the deep, restorative help you need to keep fighting the good fight.

Building Comrades

If you want to build up a group of comrades in your life, you need to be as clear as you possibly can be about the mission you are on. Maybe it's "Graduate from college with a 3.25 or higher GPA" or "Get my real estate license." It could be anything from "Stay sober for the next ninety days" to "Develop Christlike character in my kids" to "Build a thriving, intimate marriage" to "Open a T-shirt business in two years." When you take the time to articulate the small, medium, and long-term missions of your life, the comrades you need will be revealed in those who want to empathize with, resource, sharpen, and support you along the way. When you see them, you can begin connecting on purpose.

I have a mission to communicate the Word of God, equipping others to know and love Jesus through the Bible. I keep a Marco Polo (an asynchronous video messaging app where you can talk back and forth) going with two other female authors and Bible teachers. We ask each other questions about writing, editors, publishing, social media, and professional resources. We even talk about what clothing and earrings to wear to events. They pray for the weekends I teach. They know what it feels like to be a writer who suddenly has a house full of kids in the summer. We understand one another's work down to the way we spend the hours of a day. Over time our connection has become more personal, but it exists because of our work. That doesn't make it shallow or one-dimensional: it offers sharp definition. It helps me know how to enjoy the beauty of our connection in a relational world with limits.

Jesus was crystal clear about his mission, and it changed the people with whom he spent time, creating some unlikely connections that the religious leaders complained about. They objected to Jesus eating with known sinners, speaking to women, and befriending those thought to be unclean. However, Jesus knew who he came for and what he came to do. He met those criticisms with a restatement of his mission, as in Matthew 9:13 when he said in response, "Go and learn what this means: 'I desire mercy, not sacrifice.' For I have not come to call the righteous, but sinners." It isn't at all unreasonable to suspect that some of his acquaintances from the motley crew he befriended would have become part of the seventy-two who were trained by Jesus to be sent out to preach and heal. Jesus had a mission to reach sinners with the good news of repentance and forgiveness from God. Who might get excited about this and want to help spread it? The very sinners who'd received it! These "objectionable types" (and, *gasp*—women!) went on to resource and support his mission and message, even giving lavishly in gratitude.

> After this, Jesus traveled about from one town and village to another, proclaiming the good news of the kingdom of God. The Twelve were with him, and also some women who had been cured of evil spirits and diseases: Mary (called Magdalene) from whom seven demons had come out; Joanna the wife of Chuza, the manager of Herod's household; Susanna; and many others. These women were helping to support them out of their own means. (Luke 8:1–3)

As Jesus did what he came to do, others joined him. This is how you find comrades: *Do your thing*. While you are running *your* race, others will be on your right and left, on the same course and heading in the same direction, grateful for your presence, happy to encourage you if you slow down, recommending better gear, offering you a drink of water. Building comrade relationships means you each give tangibly to your shared mission. You send encouraging texts, ensure their application gets seen, teach them a needed skill, offer wise counsel, or show up when others walk away.

Comrades show themselves through service and support of your common focus. There were two men—Joseph of Arimathea and Nicodemus—who showed up after the crucifixion and death of Jesus to serve him, even when it looked like his mission had failed. They still came, loved, and helped. Joseph was called a "disciple of Jesus" (John 19:38), and Nicodemus had likely become one as well (John 3). They brought the necessary supplies to wrap and bury Jesus's body with respect, using their own resources—even providing the tomb. The dividing line between comrades and everyone else in Jesus's community was the shift *from passive to active*. Comrades don't just mentally ascend to a common set of beliefs; they move together in pursuit of how those beliefs take shape in the world.

> To the Jews who had believed him, Jesus said, "If you hold to my teaching, you are really my disciples. Then you will know the truth, and the truth will set you free." (John 8:31–32)

The best comrades are made by using common resources, growing or training together, or providing accountability for what you said you're about. Connections like this work well when your comrade is close enough to see your life but far enough away not to get lost in the weeds. You need some people who know your heart but aren't wrapped up in all your daily stuff, offering a voice to speak into your life at the right moments. This happened in my son's summer camp group last year. A group conversation about money took place among eight teenage guys who all earned minimum wage at summer jobs. One young man pushed my son to open up his own account with our church right then to start giving his own money in a tithe of his paycheck. This friend was in the same fight on the same battlefield as my son: not making much money and still growing as a man and learning how to follow Christ. We had taught our kids about tithing, but encountering the counsel and testimony of a comrade is very different than hearing it from a parent! My son has experienced life in a new place of obedience because a comrade challenged him at the right moment and offered testimony that tithing was "the best thing he's ever done with his money." You need the voice of comrades to help you move, grow, and take new ground on the same battlefield at the same time.

Choosing Comrades

You don't so much choose comrades as you *discover* them. They pop up while you go about the work that you are doing in the world or in the church. People who have similar gifts, do similar things to you, and seem to be moving in the same direction accumulate around you—at work or at school or with your marriage, family, gifts, or hobbies. The question is, who are *your* true comrades in arms? Lots of people orbit your life, as they did Jesus's, but he knew how to recognize the real ones who had the same heart for the same mission, facing the same enemy. Jesus shared that knowledge in a famous sermon called the Sermon on the Mount, in which he painted a clear picture of comrades in the kingdom of God. The whole sermon gave the marks of an ideal comrade in his Father's kingdom in heart, motivations, relationships, patterns of prayer, use of money, relationship to fear and worry, and more.

You could read it as instructions on how to live as true disciples (and it was that), but it was also a way to weed out posers—those who might *say* they were about the same mission, who might *say* they loved the same God he loved, who might *say* they knew his Father in heaven, but who truly did not. At the end of the sermon, Jesus gave three contrasts in a row to separate the people listening into two groups—*real comrades* and *fake ones*. The contrasts of two roads, two trees, and two builders helped separate people who *claimed* to be about his mission from the ones who would *actively participate* in it. You can use the same contrasts to help you discover your real comrades among all the people around you doing similar work. Ask yourself:

- **What road are they on?** Is this person truly heading the same direction as you? How did they get to where they are? Where do they want to end up?

Enter through the narrow gate. For wide is the gate and broad is the road that leads to destruction, and many enter through it. But small is the gate and narrow the road that leads to life, and only a few find it. (Matt. 7:13–14)

- **What is growing on their tree?** What fruit do you see in their life? What have they put long-term care and work into producing? What have they grown that nourishes other people?

A good tree cannot bear bad fruit, and a bad tree cannot bear good fruit. . . . Thus, by their fruit you will recognize them. (Matt. 7:18, 20)

- **What foundation are they building on?** Notice the speed, materials, and quality of what is being built in their life. Whose wisdom do they value? Whose words are they putting into practice to build their family, business, friendships, etc.?

Not everyone who says to me, "Lord, Lord," will enter the kingdom of heaven, but only the one who does the will of my Father who is in heaven. . . . Therefore everyone who hears these words of mine and puts them into practice is like a wise man who built his house on the rock. (Matt. 7:21, 24)

Jesus eventually shook off the last of his fake comrades with a particularly "offensive" teaching. He knew exactly how outrageous it would sound, but he only wanted kingdom coworkers who could accept his absolute lordship. Jesus was looking for fellow soldiers who could accept his word even when it was beyond their full understanding. So he openly taught something he knew would cause confusion and elicit rejection: "Whoever eats my flesh and drinks my blood has eternal life, and I will raise them up at the last day. For my flesh is real food and my blood is real drink. Whoever eats my flesh and drinks my blood remains in me, and I in them" (John 6:54–56). Jesus purposely showed the parts of himself that were difficult to accept and understand. "From this time many of his disciples turned back and no longer followed him" (John 6:66), but the ones who stayed were all in. Only the ones who would follow him completely as "the Holy One of God" (John 6:69) remained when others left.

Maybe you've hidden parts of yourself that you think will cause others to reject you when, in fact, exposing those things may be the way to find your true comrades. When you operate in the truth and fullness of who you are, it will reveal the people on the same road who are growing to bear the same fruit and building the same kind of life. The people Jesus chased away with his words that day were bound to leave anyway.

As I live and work, I keep my eyes open for comrades God may bring into my life by occasionally asking myself, "What are the gifts God is calling me to use right now? And how do I need to grow in those?" Some of my best comrades came into my life for a season to help me grow in my gifts or maturity. God loves to send you comrades to give you the help and courage to become all of who he made you to be. Comrades are necessary connections for support, resources, and encouragement to that end. He has sent them to me, sometimes even before I knew I needed them.

Like when I had pushed away exercising any kind of organizational leadership for many years. After I left the corporate world to work in the church, I was wary of how corporate leadership was wielded for power and promotion. I was also afraid of the baggage around women in ministry, so I decided it was best to just leave leadership behind me. For good. But then I met a comrade on the staff of my church. She'd spent many years leading at the top of the banking industry. Her no-time-like-the-present ability to make things happen made meetings with her . . . interesting. If I described a problem or barrier, she'd say, "Well, let's just go find them right now and get this taken care of." And she'd get up from her chair and expect me to follow her as she trolled the office until she tracked down the right person. Once, she even waved someone out of another meeting into the hallway to settle something right then! She liked eye contact and direct communication; long email conversations were definitely not her style. I was equal parts amused and nervous about how she led. One day I asked her, "How do you know when God wants you to lead?" She answered me without hesitation, "When it honors him and serves other people. I have learned to only lead when it's service." This was a comrade sent to me from the Lord to straighten out a few things in me.

Somehow, in all my leadership baggage and brokenness, I'd forgotten the point is to "use whatever gift you have received to serve others, as faithful stewards of God's grace in its various forms" (1 Pet. 4:10). Our gifts are there to literally pass out the grace of God to the people around us. I was so caught up in my head about the rules around leadership that I'd forgotten to ask the one simple, right question (which I still ask to this day when faced with any opportunity): "Does this honor God and serve others?" I know God sent her to pull that gift back out of me, dust it off, and start to use it in a new and better way. That's the power of a timely comrade.

Comrade Loneliness

I cry, but I wouldn't say I'm a crier. So when I found tears rolling down my own face during the first session of a conference in California, it not only took me by surprise, it also took me seventy-two hours to process *why*. The first speaker of the day was bright and winsome while tackling a controversial passage from the Old Testament about women. As she took this Scripture apart, she made me better understand God—and therefore love him more—and put a smile on my face. There was nothing sad about the teaching, but I cried through it until the woman next to me handed me tissues. That was awkward.

I didn't know how lonely I was for comrades.

I had been teaching at my church for several years and in seminary, but I didn't know any other women who wanted to dive deep into Scripture and were as convinced as I was that even the Bible passages we chafe against, when properly understood, will lead us to a deeper love of Jesus. I'd been subtly sent the message as a communicator that being "academic" and being "relatable" were completely opposite things that could not coexist. So I often felt unable to be myself, wondering if I was leaning too far in one direction or the other to touch hearts and minds with the Word of God.

It took a flight to California to see a new possibility for my work in Ohio, and it appeared through a distant comrade on an identical mission. Every penny I spent getting to that conference was worth the freedom I got from stumbling across this teacher who was both theological and *real*. What I'd been told was impossible had left me feeling alone, like I had no backup, no way to grow, and no resources to draw on for what I was doing. The loneliness from a lack of comrades felt more like being stuck and unsupported, battling low energy or discouragement in my work.

You *so* need the simple presence of comrades, even if you find one across the country. Just the presence of a comrade can lift you up! God can use comrades to encourage you that there is someone out there fighting the same fight. That day in the conference I felt understood by God. He settled a question deep down inside me that constantly asked, "Am I the only one?" The vision I had for my life and ministry was affirmed, encouraged, and clarified just by accidentally hearing this woman speak. (I've tried to meet up with her but haven't managed to do so yet. I'm hoping God will give me the opportunity to tell her this story and thank her in person one day.)

I was lonely doing my work, even though I was surrounded by other people following Christ and other kingdom coworkers. Something was set free and solidified deep within my heart, and the tears just came tumbling out of that hole in my soul. I realized about three days later how many doubts were hiding out in that empty space. I had been entertaining distracting, unhelpful thoughts like, "Maybe I heard God wrong," or "Maybe I am a little too geeky," or "Maybe there isn't a place for me or how I'm made." I went about my daily work unaware of how these thoughts were chipping away at my confidence and energy. If no one is running alongside you in your work, that kind of loneliness cannot be filled by your best friend or your husband or your parents. This layer of your soul was made for comrades who *get* the physical and spiritual mission that God has given you for your days here on earth. God has meaningful work for you to do with him, and comrades embolden you to join him and to keep going.

> **Encourage one another and build each other up**, just as in fact you are doing. (1 Thess. 5:11, emphasis added)

Your Comrades Are Your Encouragers

You need some Barnabases in your life. Barnabas might be the best example of a comrade in the Bible. His real name was Joseph, but he earned the nickname "son of encouragement" (that's the meaning of *Barnabas*). Comrades are your encouragers. They support and resource your mission in tangible and intangible ways. Barnabas was gifted by the Spirit to support the earliest apostolic leaders of the church as they preached the gospel. God gave him a knack for seeing and understanding where his grace was moving so he could lift people up with resources and momentum at critical moments. The impact of great comrades is foundational to every mission. As you have (and become) a comrade, the impact of your work will be multiplied.

The first mention of Barnabas is at a time when the church was experiencing a great move of the Spirit of God:

> With great power the apostles continued to testify to the resurrection of the Lord Jesus. And God's grace was so powerfully at work in them all that there were no needy persons among them. . . . A Levite from Cyprus, whom the apostles called Barnabas (which means "son of encouragement"), sold a field he owned and brought the money and put it at the apostles' feet. (Acts 4:33–34, 36–37)

Barnabas was one of the first to recognize what the Spirit was doing and join God in his work. Great comrades in your life will recognize and resource where they see God taking you. Sometimes it is with just their presence, and other times with very specific actions or words. I wrote an Acknowledgments page in my first book, *How to Stay Standing*, to say thank you to the "incredible women that God has used for wisdom, counsel, help, strengthening, encouragement, and comfort as this book was being written. . . . Each of you met me in a tiny moment that ended up being huge."

That's what comrades do: they intercept your fight in the small moments. When you look back and consider their impact, it is always much bigger than you realized in the moment. No mission moves forward without comrades on the battlefield.

Barnabas played this role again at a critical point in the life of Saul (later referred to as Paul) after Saul had a dramatic encounter with the resurrected Jesus and became a whole-hearted believer. Because he'd previously hated Christians, trying to have them arrested or killed, no one trusted Saul's conversion. No one except Barnabas. Barnabas was the one who recognized the genuine work of the Lord in Saul and took him to the next place in his mission:

> When [Saul] came to Jerusalem, he tried to join the disciples, but they were all afraid of him, not believing that he really was a disciple. But Barnabas took him and brought him to the apostles. He told them how Saul on his journey had seen the Lord and that the Lord had spoken to him, and how in Damascus he had preached fearlessly in the name of Jesus. (Acts 9:26–27)

Barnabas walked by his side for a season into what was next, putting his own reputation on the line to encourage Saul in the work God had for him. Barnabas played the role of a true comrade for Saul again when God brought the gospel to a city called Antioch. He was sent to investigate the strange reports of the Holy Spirit coming to gentiles. (Until this moment the church had spread as a sect of the Jewish faith, and the apostles didn't expect gentiles to be included.) Barnabas was a trusted comrade to many in the church, so they sent him to verify this new front in the fight to spread the gospel. Great comrades often have the perfect marriage of a shared mission and the distance sometimes needed for clarity.

> When [Barnabas] arrived and saw what the grace of God had done, he was glad and encouraged them all to remain true to the Lord with all their hearts. He was a good man, full of the Holy Spirit and faith, and a great number of people were brought to the Lord. (Acts 11:23–24)

Barnabas not only saw what God was doing, he also knew what was needed for the momentum to continue. In this case? They needed Saul! "Then Barnabas went to Tarsus to look for Saul, and when he found him, he brought him to Antioch. So for a whole year Barnabas and Saul met with the church and taught great numbers of people. The disciples were called Christians first at Antioch" (Acts 11:25–26). Can you imagine how much this would have emboldened Saul at that time? After having been doubted and even rejected, he was sought out by the guy everyone trusted. God used Barnabas as a key comrade for many of his chosen leaders because Barnabas saw where God was moving and came alongside them to *embolden their calling and work*. You don't have to conjure up your own encouragement: God can send you the Barnabases your soul needs.

Who Are Your Comrades?

Comrades come in a delightful and wide variety, so let's consider them from a few different angles. Who are your obvious ones (like Jesus's Mary, Martha, and Lazarus)? The few who are barely outside your circle, probably only due to misaligned

105

circumstances. You love them so much, but your access is limited. Who is that in your life? Write down their names on the blueprint.

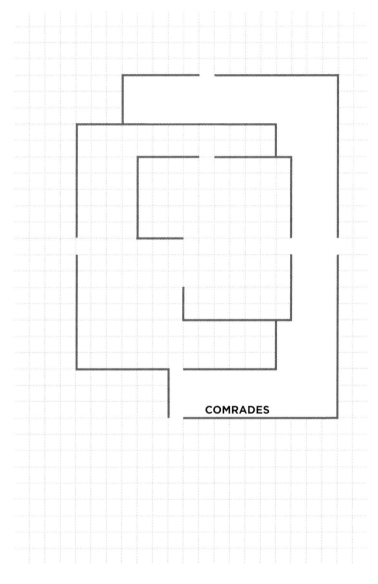

COMRADES

Who is jogging alongside you for a project or an interval with a specific reason right now? Some comrades are runners who come along for just a part of your marathon course. These people have clearly shown up during the current season of your life or work. Add their names to your design.

Who trains, equips, or stands by you in the fights you're fighting right now? Those who are on the battlefield but not necessarily in all your daily business make great comrades! Write down their names.

Some comrades may be people you receive from as they run ahead on your course. Who comes to mind as a comrade from this angle? Add their names as possible comrades too.

Do you see anyone who might be moving into or out of this part of your relational world? Maybe they've been part of your circle but life circumstances are changing. Our relationships are ever-changing, so don't be afraid to acknowledge movement. One person in my current circle started years ago in my community, then became a comrade when a mutual friend said, "Hey, you guys live near each other and you're both about to have a baby—you should meet!" We'd meet for a run or at the park with our kids, and we quickly realized we were already comrades: we were both moms and Jesus lovers and were serving at the same church, raising kids the same age, and committed to kingdom impact in our local township and schools. After a brief time, the deeper territory of the circle was natural, as we had crossover activities, shared missions, a high affinity, and easy weekly access. She moved from a comrade into my circle and has stayed there ever since.

If you have someone moving into/out of your comrades, jot down their name here for more consideration.

As you look back at the names you wrote (or didn't write), take a few minutes and talk to God using the words of a prayer Jesus prayed for all believers in John 17. His desire was for his people to be on mission together, unified in spreading life, light, and the good news of the kingdom of God. Use these phrases and pray for God to multiply the comrades in your life and encourage you in your work.

- Father, at the end of my life I want to say, "I have brought you glory on earth by finishing the work you gave me to do" (v. 4). Please bring me the right comrades in this season for the work I'm doing and for the work you want me to do.
- Help me to recognize these people by the easy give-and-take we have together, our common language, and our same heart for the work of our hands—just as Jesus felt about his disciples when he said, "For I gave them the words you gave me and they accepted

them" (v. 8). Show me who around me accepts me and is on the same road.

- I feel alone and vulnerable sometimes, Lord. I need you to bring comrades into my life for protection, teamwork, and comfort as I go. I'm asking, as Jesus requested for his comrades, that for me and mine you "protect them . . . that they may be one as we are one" (v. 11).

- Most of all, Father, I want to be with you, and I know your Spirit resides in your people. So I need to stay connected to your people. Please bring others to me who desire life with you: "I want those you have given me to be with me where I am" (v. 24). Please build comrades into my life to encourage me as I try to follow you. Amen.

The next part of Jesus's relational world was his **community**. It is larger and varied, similar to a group of comrades, but Jesus spent a lot of his ministry differentiating between kingdom comrades and the rest of his Jewish community. Your community is a big network of the people who have formed your soul throughout your personal history. I suspect in the next chapter you will find a little baggage and a lot of beauty—or maybe a lot of baggage and a little beauty. Either way, come with me to consider how you were and are formed *in community* and what part of your soul deeply needs these relationships today.

Live Welcomed by a Community

As we have opportunity, let us do good to all people, especially to those who belong to the family of believers.

Galatians 6:10

Susan's door was right across the hallway in our first apartment building. She helped me reset a blown fuse in our old building and then showed up a couple months later with leftovers to watch the first episode of *Survivor*. We helped each other drag things to the dumpster and climb the stairs with groceries. We laughed about the manager of our building, who was always on his balcony smoking pot instead of fixing things. Eventually we trusted each other enough to offer advice for just about any part of our lives. I still remember the birth of her first daughter and the evening her husband accidentally blew up a box of fireworks in their basement. We don't see each other often now, but our connection made an imprint on my life. If I rang her doorbell today, she'd let me in with a smile. In one sense our relationship is in the past, but she is part of the life of my soul in the section of my blueprint called **community**.

Community is a mixed network of all the people you've picked up just living your life. The people in this realm aren't as strategically connected to a specific purpose or mission as comrades are. This section of your blueprint isn't just one cohesive group; rather, it's made up of groups and individuals with whom *you* are the common denominator. They are both past and present, family and non-family, inside or outside of your faith. The word *community* as discussed in this chapter is the invisible web of people from your life that you have gathered through *external* circumstances. Some may have had significant internal impact and are very beloved, while others may stay a "friendly" arm's length for many years in this realm. I used to define my community as my "Christmas card list," but since I haven't sent cards in a few years, I guess I can't say that anymore. If I run into someone in my community, I usually leave saying, "Let's get together!" I always mean it, but the truth is they take up more room in my heart than on my calendar.

My people vary from "basketball moms" to college friends, from neighbors to my hair stylist, from coworkers at church to my brothers, from my kids' teachers to "friends of friends." As time goes on, we likely won't sustain close friendship or strategic mission, but community remains a large part of my relational world, an important piece of building a life I love.

By the time I was thirty, I could see that most relationships turn out to be seasonal in nature, meaning they come into my life for a specific time and then naturally fade. However, it took me another decade to truly see and value the vast web of community that gets created as that happens. My personal tendency is to focus on my core and circle and overlook the part of my soul that only thrives in the context of a sur-rounding community.

There are moments that the presence of this often-invisible realm of community comes into sharp focus. One of those for me is at a local 5k race. Every year, everyone in our town-ship comes out in support of the local school district for an annual fundraiser. This year my son sang the national an-them with his chorus, my daughters ran with their running club and track team, my other son gathered a group of guys from different area high schools to run, my husband greeted clients of his law firm on the course, and I couldn't make it ten feet without chatting with someone from the gym, the church, or the schools. When part of my community comes out of the woodwork at this event, I appreciate the *geographic* web of relationships I live in year-round. I can't always see it together in one place, but this network creates an ongoing sense that I belong somewhere. I just happen to catch a glimpse every May. My township is part of this chapter of my life, so geographic community is a layer in this part of my blueprint.

Community is a mixture of people, past and present, who have shaped your life, story, and soul. As you think through your community, these are the people who attach you to both who you've been and who you are becoming. Maybe you hold tightly to every relationship you've had. You're drowning in so many people you can't seem to manage this realm of your life without feeling bad you can't see everyone. I'm the op-posite. In the past, I didn't understand the value or practices of maintaining community, so when I would begin a new phase of life, I just cut people off and moved on to make room for new relationships. I unnecessarily lived as though anyone I couldn't see regularly couldn't stay in my life. I have never once visited a college friend just for fun or gone back to a high school reunion or (until very recently) made any meaningful effort to keep hold of friends who move away. I told myself I was just good at "leaving the past in the past," but I think I was a little *too* good at it.

For many years, I overlooked a significant sense of belonging available to me, blind to the richness of living in community. I operated on the belief that relationships are only valuable if they are in the more definable spaces of core, circle, or comrades. But God creates a beautiful variety of people to enjoy who can surround you with refreshment, blessing, support, and love as you move through life. These community relationships matter to the thriving of your soul, telling pieces of the story of where you are and where you've been.

My first experience with feeling something like community was inside my extended family. I got trash bags full of hand-me-downs from third cousins. On Thanksgiving night I'd lay awake in my sleeping bag listening to twenty or so people play cards, including Aunt So-and-So who was "once removed" and definitely not my aunt. There was a sense of belonging, even if I wasn't sure how I was related to them all. As my life went on, most of these relationships faded into the past, but the sense of community belonging lingered. I grew up knowing there were a bunch of people in the world who would welcome me simply because I was "Bernie's daughter." That's what a community does best: **a community welcomes you**. There may be moments, times, or seasons when you're physically together, but when you're not, the sense of hospitality lingers even many years later. I think of it as the collection of doors I could knock on, confident I'll be welcomed by the person on the other side.

One of those doors for me is in Indiana at Becky's house—even though I've never been there. Becky moved away years ago from the city where I knew her. I love seeing her smiling face in pictures. I held her kids as infants, but they wouldn't know me now. I love thinking about her a state away, still getting her Diet Cokes only from a soda fountain—never a can or two-liter! She intersected my life many years ago, just before I hit rock bottom, and stayed near me through it, eventually seeing the light ahead with me as well. After long gaps we still communicate, and I'd say we are friends, but that word feels more like someone in my present *circle*. I think the better one for us is now *community*. Old friends are a wonderful part of your community, and she is a beloved part of mine, present and past. I am still welcome with her and she with me.

Jesus grew up in a community too, one that shared his hometown, history, language, and culture. Today, it doesn't seem strange to us that someone's job or passion might take them away from their hometown and extended family, but in Jesus's culture, it was almost unheard of. The family provided for a person's livelihood and survival; you didn't just leave. When Jesus stepped into his calling to earthly ministry from his heavenly Father, a clear distinction became apparent in his life between his kingdom coworkers and his Jewish extended family. It was the line between comrades and community. John makes it very clear that Jesus's brothers were on the community side of that line even just six months before his death on the cross. John stated at this time that "even his own brothers did not believe in him" (John 7:5).

A lack of belief in his identity and mission meant that they could not be comrades: Jesus's ministry immediately repositioned most of his family into the realm of community. He separated the two different kinds of relationships again and again. He never claimed his cultural or familial ties were unimportant; he just inserted a clear line between those who supported his kingdom mission and those connected to his life in other ways. His comrades were closer than blood or history. But his Jewish family was very welcome to become comrades! The biblical record shows that at least one brother became a true believer.

In 1 Corinthians 15:7, his earthly brother, James, is named as one Jesus appeared to after the resurrection. We cannot be sure what pushed James across the line into true belief (though a visit from beyond the grave would probably have done it!). We know, however, that he *did* make the shift. James became the leader of the early church in Jerusalem after the resurrection until he was martyred in 62 CE. He came to have a deep faith that his own brother was the Messiah, choosing *comrade* as his primary identity in the Epistle of James when he called himself a "servant of God and of the Lord Jesus Christ" (James 1:1), entirely skipping over his lesser identity as a "brother from the same mother" on earth. Family and community are good gifts, but James came to understand what this blueprint reflects: camaraderie in the kingdom is the closer realm of connection. James made the move from the community of kin to comrades in the kingdom with his brother Jesus.

Aside from old friends and extended family members, there are all kinds of other places to establish and build community connections. School and work usually create the highest quantity because you spend so many of your waking hours physically present in these locations. Perhaps some other places could be on your street, like I found. For years, I'd walk down to my neighbor's house to help supervise the chaos of hosting all the kids on the street, since mine were four of them! We'd end up sitting for many hours together, eating too much candy corn out of her big glass pumpkin in the fall. A growing sense of community connection was a natural result of the hours I spent on her driveway and in her kitchen. It feels natural to build community with the people right around you. We are relational to our very core, so we tend to spin webs of community wherever we spend time.

Building Community

Building and keeping the kind of belonging found in community is not complicated, but it does have to be intentional. The good news is that very small things can keep a sense of healthy belonging growing in these kinds of relationships. Even a low investment can build a stronger network into your life if you simply make the shift to *intention*. Community can feel like it just "happens" because of our relational makeup, but you can also grow and strengthen it on purpose. Goodness knows I'm no authority on how to do this, but I can certainly testify to the emptiness in part of your soul that comes from *not* being intentional. I've learned the simplest rule of thumb for a stronger community is to *show up* and *do good*. It sounds so simple, but when life consumes us, it's easy to toss aside even these two simple things that result in communal belonging.

Presence is the simplest and biggest way to build community. In the busy era of my life raising four kids, I am most tempted not to show up. Time is precious, and I can sometimes hoard it for myself instead of using it to build community. I also have a personality where I need to recharge with time alone, so if I'm running near empty, it never sounds great to me to gather with others. However, showing up where your community is present is a big deal—even for introverts or people who'd rather get their to-do lists done for the day. Alone time and checked boxes have never resulted in a greater sense of relational connection, yet I'm tempted to always do those things first.

These tendencies caught up with me after Covid when I was no longer required to be in the office a certain amount of time. Since a lot of the hands-on work I do requires research and writing, silence is my friend! And I like it. So I began to mostly work at home, only showing up for critical meetings. Within a year I began to feel very distant from my staff community. I would walk into meetings and the loss of belonging was so evident. About six months ago, after several years working at home, I switched back to a predictable in-office schedule. My sense of warm, connected community with the staff has skyrocketed. Because I am *present*. When you show up you keep a pathway open for God to provide for you, bless you, comfort and delight you, give you resources for your life and work—not to mention keep your soul whole and healthy with an everyday sense of companionship and belonging.

Because you find people for your community in so many places, you just need to ask where your people are present . . . and go there. I know how simplistic that sounds, but I call it "the ministry of *presence*." Showing up definitely builds community. Friday night football games are a big deal at my kids' school, so even with no kid on the team we started showing up. I don't always want to go, but my kids do, and I end up seeing all kinds of people in my community—my husband's partners or associates, local business owners, teachers, parents I love, the local Young Life leaders, and many others. When I am present I have quick exchanges that make me aware of what's going on with them, such as an injury, a spouse who is traveling a lot, or a big promotion. It's amazing what you learn in the snack bar line! (And I let myself leave at halftime because I didn't really come for the game.)

The other very simple way to build a sense of belonging with a community is to *do good to the people right in front of you.* You may not see everyone in your community even monthly, but when you do, ask yourself, "How can I show them favor? Preference? Give or share with them generously?" You will "reap a harvest" of blessing in your life from genuinely doing good to the people who are regularly in your path: your neighbors, coworkers, old friends, kids' teachers—whoever you consider your community.

> Let us not become weary in doing good, for at the proper time we will reap a harvest if we do not give up. Therefore, as we have opportunity, let us do good to all people, especially to those who belong to the family of believers. (Gal. 6:9–10)

The harvest of blessing comes when you eventually discover that your simple goodness to others has strengthened your network into people of peace, gratitude, and goodwill who are genuinely in your corner. The next time you are in need, it may very well be your community that comes through for you. I've seen it over and over: communities are *so* good at activating help and provision and blessing in one another's lives for concrete, specific, tangible needs. The early church community was known for exactly this. They were in a time of growing from hundreds into thousands, coming from different backgrounds, some gentiles and some Jews, some barely grasping the gospel, others steeped in Jewish Scriptures. They were definitely not a bunch of besties, but by the grace of God, they did good to one another.

> No one claimed that any of their possessions was their own, but they shared everything they had. . . . God's grace was so powerfully at work in them all that there were no needy persons among them. For from time to time those who owned land or houses sold them, brought the money from the sales and put it at the apostles' feet, and it was distributed to anyone who had need. (Acts 4:32–35)

Jesus did this too. He often healed, delivered, or encouraged someone just because he *could*.

> On a Sabbath Jesus was teaching in one of the synagogues, and a woman was there who had been crippled by a spirit for eighteen years. She was bent over and could not straighten up at all. When Jesus saw her, he called her forward and said to her, "Woman, you are set free from your infirmity." Then he put his hands on her, and immediately she straightened up and praised God. (Luke 13:10–13)

There is no indication that Jesus anticipated running into that woman at the synagogue. He simply saw her and gave her what he had to offer that day their paths crossed. He healed many people within his Jewish community in a similar way—including a man born blind in John 9 and a man with a shriveled hand in Mark 3:1–5—just to generously share the blessings of his kingdom.

Where will you be today? What do you have in your pocket or purse? What kind of business do you run? What food did you make last night? Simple things bring such blessing. I saw community grow in the bleachers at a basketball game when a woman walked into the high school gym and, after a quick glance around, walked up to my group of basketball mom friends. She said quietly, "Ladies, there is a young woman in the bathroom in desperate need of some feminine hygiene products. Surely one of you has something to help her out, right?" In about fifteen seconds we offered far more than she could have ever needed. Although, admittedly, this is somewhat less spiritual than healing a shriveled hand, we still loved being provision for another woman and knowing we helped someone just because we *could*. God can use anything at your fingertips that you're willing to share in order to increase your sense of community with the people right around you every day.

Community is built when we do this in everyday moments. So, buy their coffee. Say the compliment out loud. Send a meal to someone who is sick. My husband always insists I say yes to all the neighbor kids when they come knocking on the door for their baseball or Girl Scout fundraisers, selling overpriced popcorn or wrapping paper or coupon books I'll never use. He always tells me, "Just do it! Good neighbors are worth an extra ten dollars for bad popcorn." He's right. And the opposite is also true: nothing kills community like a handwritten note in your mailbox from your neighbor asking for twenty dollars because your little boy ran over a plant on his Big Wheel. (A plant that was still very much alive.) I still remember that after seventeen years because a lack of generosity feels like the opposite of the spirit of community.

I have experienced so much goodness through community—kindnesses left on my doorstep, professional connections, an appointment with a specific doctor who helped my child. I truly do see it as an avenue through which God cares for me—even financially! I had to order a custom blind for an odd-shaped window in my daughter's bedroom. I had no idea a window treatment could be so expensive! So I called Budget Blinds. The man who showed up at my house to measure turned out to be a member of my church. As he was writing up the order, he announced with a wink that he was giving me the Friends & Family rate because we were family in Christ. He used his resources to bless me that day. He showed me the goodness of God in a unique way that touched me, and he didn't hesitate to do it. Community is so good at blessing through the sharing of resources.

Something inside you comes alive when you do good to others: it has the power to infuse any random day with more purpose. You can't put each person on your calendar every week as you do with your circle, but you can go to where they gather. You won't necessarily share a kingdom mission as you do with your comrades, but you can be a soul-satisfying blessing whenever possible. You are made to be part of the beauty and generosity in the life of a community.

Maintaining Community

If you want community, you have to do something that can seem counterintuitive: resist the urge to try to pull these people into closer relationship. If you don't, community can feel overwhelming to maintain. So many women struggle with an inflated sense of obligation to always pursue deeper relationships, feeling constantly disappointed at the lack of time to maintain sufficient closeness with everyone they know. If you think you owe someone *more* every time you interact, eventually you'll be exhausted or discouraged. The beauty of community is that it doesn't require that for maintenance. Instead, these relationships thrive with a few commitments and a few boundaries that preserve the joy of community. That joy evaporates when you overextend yourself. Obligation always backfires in community.

Jesus moved through his community relationships committed to *possibility* but never *obligation*. He never forced relationships closer. Jesus's interactions with individuals in his community were often onetime blessings as he simply shared, instructed, or gave to people in the families and towns in which he lived and worked. Jesus didn't seem to feel at all guilty for not being best buddies with everyone he met. I imagine him just smiling and moving on with his day. He saw, he blessed, he kept moving. It is not realistic—nor God's intention—for you to deepen every relationship you have. It's okay to simply be good to someone you know and leave it at that.

If an interaction led someone closer to his ongoing mission, Jesus was always open to anyone becoming a comrade. Community is a great place to discover comrades, but to make this transition you need to be clear about your mission: What are you pursuing in your life right now? Can this person truly be a part of that? Or do you just feel bad saying no to a request for coffee? Your time and capacity for relationships are limited. When you accept all invitations or bend to the expectations someone else puts on your relationship, you will give away those precious resources to deepen connections that don't necessarily serve God's purposes in your life. Jesus beautifully maintained community with a simple pattern: when he saw an opportunity, he said yes to being a blessing and continued on his way.

Seeing the chance to bless your community can be a challenge. Life moves fast and is always very full! Sometimes I struggle to see the everyday chances I have to build or maintain community. I've discovered a few easy things that help me keep my eyes open to my community:

1. **Pray for the people in your community.** I put a list of names inside my bathroom mirror to remind me of people I don't see as often. I see this list when I brush my teeth or wash my face. The names aren't of my best friends but of people I may not think of as often. Right now, the names are a mom I know from school, a friend of my son's, and a neighbor. When I pray for people by name, I'm naturally more sensitive to their needs. I might think to send a quick text or seek them out in a crowd and ask how they are. The Holy Spirit can reveal needs and connect people when you pray.

2. **Have a regular spot.** Maybe your spot is at the university commons, the neighborhood coffee shop, or wherever the local band is playing on Saturday night. My husband and I go to the same restaurant whenever we sneak out for a weekday meal together, and now we know one of the waiters. We always try to leave a big tip for him. Wherever it is, showing up to the same place on purpose will increase your sense of belonging to the people there. Pick a spot and go fairly often.

3. **Make small talk.** I'm not gonna lie, this one kills me
   a little. I historically hate small talk, as any of my
   friends can tell you. There is a long-standing joke
   from an old small group of mine because I lost it one
   night when someone insisted we do an icebreaker
   after we'd been meeting for four years. I rolled my
   eyes and gave a little speech about how we only had
   an hour and it was a waste of time. That speech has
   been brought up many times in the years since. I have
   always found (what I saw as) "fluff and chatter" an-
   noying. So I can't believe I am actually saying this,
   but it turns out small talk has a legitimate place in
   maintaining community. There's actual research.

   Our experiences during the Covid era provided
   lots of personal evidence for this as well. When we
   were cut off from all small talk because of shelter-in-
   place orders and remote work, there was a lot more
   missing than "meaningless" conversation. Our lack
   of small talk completely shattered what some sociol-
   ogists call *weak ties* to our communities. People like
   me—who didn't think those weaker ties held together
   by chitchat mattered much—found out otherwise.
   While working remotely had its benefits, eliminating
   every hallway conversation meant we knew significantly less about people's lives. I didn't know about
   the new dog. I couldn't pray for the sick baby or vote
   on the color someone should paint their bathroom. I
   even missed out on organizational information that
   gets passed in casual exchanges.

   Small talk ties us to networks of relationships. And
   not just at work, but also in your geographic community. You will feel a greater sense of connection

in your apartment building, town, block, or neighborhood through what seems like inconsequential exchanges in the grocery line or at a local restaurant waiting for a table. God can provide so much more than I thought through this small channel: humor on a bad day, a wink of understanding, a word of encouragement, or even direction from the Holy Spirit. These one-off conversations have the power to reassure us in the unnamed places of our soul that we are seen and we are not moving through life alone. Over time, small talk plays a role in living less lonely.

Community Loneliness

We are souls who need community, and when we don't have it, the type of loneliness we feel is something no other relationships can address. Because I didn't understand this, I made a big mistake when I went to college: I cut off my entire community of the previous twelve years. I'd grown up, first grade through high school graduation, in the same town and drastically underestimated the role that community played in my overall feeling of belonging when I left for college. Because a new phase of life was beginning, I thought the right thing to do was cut off everyone from home and throw myself completely into my new place. Now it seems very severe, but I rejected rides and roommates and coffees with anyone from my hometown. I wanted to be on my own and start fresh. It wasn't hard because in the early '90s there were no smartphones with tweets, snaps, texts, or videos keeping me digitally connected to the lives of those in my community. I would have had to make a long-distance phone call, plan a face-to-face visit, or send an actual letter. With a stamp!

I didn't do any of those things. I mistakenly thought the only relationships I should focus on in my life were the ones in my future—the new ones I was about to make. This belief caused me to feel much lonelier than I needed to. I didn't think I needed people to hold my hand through a change in life season, so I made a sharp, purposeful separation: I cut the safety net of community. Even though I loved my hometown friends, I quickly lost touch. I could have allowed so much more of God's grace, comfort, and help to flow into my new beginning. I was very lonely in my first semesters of college because I created a chasm between my new phase and my previous one. Community could have helped to fill that, but I wouldn't let it. Community is a conduit of God's grace as life ebbs and flows, tying us to some people from our past and adding new ones in our present phases and places. Community grounds us in a sense of belonging that we can carry with us.

Sometimes the reason we experience the loss of community is not because we reject them—as I did—but because they reject us. Souls are easily damaged by this kind of rejection. Jesus knew the experience of being doubted and rejected. He knew what it meant to have his community not believe in who he really was.

> Coming to his hometown, he began teaching the people in their synagogue, and they were amazed. "Where did this man get this wisdom and these miraculous powers?" they asked. "Isn't this the carpenter's son? Isn't his mother's name Mary, and aren't his brothers James, Joseph, Simon and Judas? Aren't all his sisters with us? Where then did this man get all these things?" And they took offense at him.
>
> But Jesus said to them, "A prophet is not without honor except in his own town and in his own home." And he did

not do many miracles there because of their lack of faith. (Matt. 13:54–58)

All the way to the cross, Jesus encountered parts of his Jewish community who were unwilling to recognize his identity as the Son of God. John the Baptist called this out as Jesus first started his ministry, saying, "Among you stands one whom you do not recognize" (John 1:26 NET). Jesus existed as part of a people who did not necessarily understand or accept his identity and mission. Familiarity can sometimes lead to blindness as God matures you into the fullness of who you are, creating a sense of loneliness in your life from those who are supposed to see and know you. This is the very reason Jesus always made a distinction between comrades and community, knowing they occupied distinct spaces in the blueprint of his relational world.

Your Community Is Your Net

From the very first day of our lives to the last, we have a deep need to connect with other people in community. In the blueprint of your existing relational world, community entwines your past, present, and future, tying knots and forming an invisible web of people around your life. I picture community as a net. It's a large group of people that gets tied together one person at a time, growing in size and strength over time. The corporate idea of "networking" is a worldly echo of this idea (and also something I was terrible at in my corporate years!). Intentional "networking" connections always felt a bit false or forced, but it's certainly true that a strong network will provide support and opportunities for your work or career. Community operates best with a similar goal: *to be a constant support and offer extra capacity for help when you need it.* Your net of community should add strength and wisdom, step up when you need them, and act as an avenue for God to provide blessing in your life.

Or community can do the opposite.

Thinking of community *as a net* brings to mind two contrasting pictures in the Bible: nets can be a *trap* or a *tool.* Community can become either as well! The goal of a growing community is to stay tied to the ones who support, bless, or shape you—the people who help you thrive—or those for whom you are called to do the same.

Nets can be traps that ensnare. Getting caught up with false, empty community that isn't interested in your good will quite literally land you in traps that Satan sets in your life. Ones like David writes about in Psalm 140:4–5 when he says, "Keep me safe, LORD, from the hands of the wicked; protect me from the violent, who devise ways to trip my feet. The arrogant have hidden a snare for me; they have spread out the cords of their net and have set traps for me along my path." This kind of community practically guarantees that you will not thrive. Are your feet ensnared by people dragging you away from God along your path? Are you hanging out with people who keep you tied to things that should not be in your life? When the nation of Israel came into the promised land that God gave to them, there were people groups he told them to drive out *for their long-term good.* He knew they would not fully separate themselves from these communities and therefore sent them a warning through an angel, saying, "They will become traps for you, and their gods will become snares to you" (Judg. 2:3). Some people just can't stay tied into your life.

Nets are also tools for thriving. Nets were a key resource in the occupations of local Jewish fishermen, including a handful of Jesus's disciples. Nets were for catching fish. Jesus used a fishing analogy when he called disciples to a life following him. He said they would now be catching people instead of fish. They would still need a net! But this time it was the net of their community. The disciples learned how to work together, to find and bring in the "fish," by making more and more people a part of communities to live and grow together. Nets also need maintaining—cleaning, mending, tying back together. As you examine your net of community, are there holes that need mending through forgiveness or reconciliation? Through telling truth or confession? I willfully cut holes in my own net when I severed relationships from home as I left for college. Those holes tore at my sense of belonging. Rips and tears do happen as we live, but at least I try not to cut them myself now. A well-maintained net helps our souls thrive. As embodied souls we experience a deeper sense of belonging as our net of community is woven together over a lifetime. Community forms a sense of belonging and hospitality in our lives. The continuing presence of community is a net that ties us to the people of our past, present, and those who may be used by God to open doors for the future.

Who Is Your Community?

As you've read this chapter, who has come to mind as people in your community? Think of your home, school, family, and work, both past and present.

Add names to the blueprint, considering these questions:

Who are the people from your *past* that you consider part of your community? Who are you thankful to have known in the past? Old friends or connections? People who have shaped you in various ways?

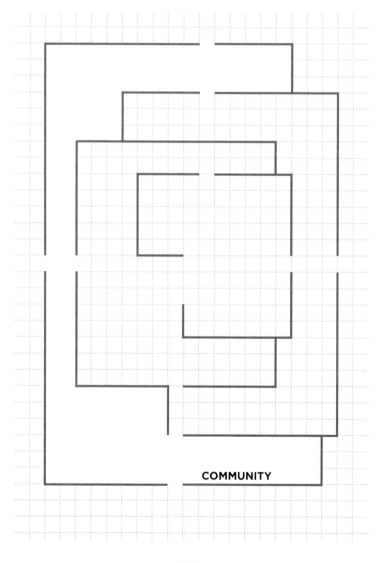

COMMUNITY

Now think about people to whom you are connected in the *present*: coworkers, neighbors, teachers, friends. Who blesses you or makes you laugh? Who leaves you feeling encouraged anytime you get to cross their path? Write their names on the blueprint.

Who in your family belongs in your community? Your family deserves special prayer and consideration as you think about your blueprint design. Most of mine have settled in this community part of my blueprint. I know the complexities as you think through family relationships. Here's a short prayer if you're wrestling with how to think about your family within your core, circle, comrades, and community. Pray for them and then write down any family names that you think belong in your community.

Lord, give me eyes to see and ears to hear the truth about my family relationships. Show me the ones that I have prioritized too much or too little. Walk with me into ones that can grow or be reconciled. Free me from any expectations and guilt others have placed on me. I want your guidance for the place of my family in my life today. You know my past, my hurt, and my capacity in this season. Please connect me to healthy community by your grace. Amen.

Who has been in your community but places doubt or obstacles in your path? People can become hindrances to what God is doing in our lives. Does anyone come to mind? Jot down names in the box below to think about as you read the chapter on **counterfeits** and evaluate whether they should remain in your community.

There is one more layer of relationship that forms our human soul. It feels completely different from the rest but is such an exciting part of human relationships. Clear your mind and get ready to consider your *crowds*. I'm willing to bet that the crowd holds much more positive possibility for your life and your soul than you might think!

Live Expectant in the Crowd

When he saw the crowds, he had compassion on them, because they were harassed and helpless, like sheep without a shepherd.

Matthew 9:36

The same forty-four Taylor Swift songs played in my car for six months. My kids insisted that any self-respecting Swiftie needed to know every single lyric to the setlist for her concert, and they were relentless. While I will admit Taylor has more variety than I had previously appreciated, just once I wanted to get in my car and *not* know what playlist would come on. Sometimes, for the life of a soul, it's good to *not* know what's coming.

The world created by God for living our external lives is a clue to what kinds of things might bring life to our internal worlds—and therefore deeply into our souls. If the weather in Ohio is any indication, he wants to keep us guessing a little! It could be eighty or forty-five degrees on October 1 and twenty-eight or seventy-eight degrees on April 1. While there could be a white Christmas, it could also be a day to play outside in just a sweatshirt. We have four predictable seasons but very unpredictable weather. The natural world is full of the juxtaposition of highly predictable elements alongside ever-changing variety. Even atoms, our basic building block of matter, have a clear particle structure but also produce very unpredictable free radicals. We seem to be designed to hold security, safety, and rhythm in tension with variety and surprise. This tension keeps us engaged in a life that is always unfolding.

You need this in relationships too. Your core will rarely change: they provide the stability of unconditional commitment that steadies you. But you also need *the crowds*: on the other end of the relational spectrum, they are the widest and most changing part of your relational blueprint. Your life can be better off because of strangers whose paths you cross even in completely unpredictable times and places. Can you imagine how dull life would be if you knew everyone you were ever going to know at the moment of your birth? Yawn. Crowds introduce an element of unfolding adventure that brings life to your soul. Dealing with people in your crowds also gives you the opportunity to expand the purpose of your life and practice love as you live. We all need the love of our rock-solid core, *and* we were made to expand in the curiosity and hopefulness of new relationships in the **crowd**. Your soul needs to wake up to days that contain new possibility, and God often brings that through new people. Crowds help you live a more *expectant* life.

But our crowds are slipping away.

We have started to devalue and minimize our interaction with all kinds of crowds, and it's going to cost us something we can't fully see yet. I started considering what crowds offer because I've never been a big fan of them—they tend to contain both strangers and large numbers of people, which is not my personal recipe for joy. Going to an FC Cincinnati soccer game last year only verified my instinct to steer clear of them. My daughters and I walked up to the stadium about a minute before game time, just as a thunderstorm broke open above us. By the time we climbed the stairs sopping wet, all the seats had been cleared due to lightning, so fifteen thousand people got shoved into the walkway around TQL Stadium where the bathrooms and concessions are. We joined the crush and quickly realized no one could move.

For an hour we got shoved around in throngs of people who inched along. It became harder and harder to stay with my girls. One woman tried to push her way between us, and I didn't use my sweetest tone of voice with her. I'm not claustrophobic, but I was pretty close to a freak-out. I touched more skin and smelled more beer breath than anyone should have to and began to wonder what would happen if someone had any kind of emergency. This was the worst kind of crowd.

Sometimes the crowds of your life do occur in large groups in one physical location, but in this chapter the meaning of *crowds* is broader than that. By crowds I simply mean the vast number of people—mostly strangers—who orbit your life online or in person. What makes them part of your crowd is not first their physical location: it's that you have *no ongoing relationship.* These are all the people in your life whom you see, pass by, or briefly interact with but share no significant personal connection when you intersect.

The Covid era rewrote our cultural narrative about physical crowds, making them unappealing, even dangerous. I notice that many now avoid anyone they don't absolutely have to interact with *as a lifestyle choice.* The changes we collectively made to our habits and practices with crowds have minimized them in our minds, and since we don't see any short-term impact of missing strangers, many of us don't really care. We stopped visiting grocery stores and can now get just about anything delivered without seeing another human. We stopped attending large events. We stopped going out to bars and restaurants. Masks killed elective, casual conversation because it was so exhausting to even be clearly heard—so most of us just pick up our phones instead of having small talk. Thankfully, not all these practices lasted beyond that couple-year period, but the societal interest and motivation to stay present and engaged among the crowds of our lives was permanently altered.

Covid shrunk our in-person crowd involvement, and it also accelerated the shift to online crowds in our increasingly digital lives. The biggest crowds are now on social media, which means they are not truly crowds. These large groups online end up being curated to your tastes and interests, which means you don't have to deal with the wide variety of people out there in the world because you can now design your online crowds to contain only demographics, interests, or opinions you like. Moving crowds primarily online has reduced them to echo chambers—just extensions of people who are more or less like your own community. And if we want to avoid someone? No problem: you can do it with one click. We are growing less able to manage our actions and feelings in the real, mixed crowds of life. I began to notice my kids needed to be taught subtle skills that I picked up much earlier in my life: how to converse face-to-face with new people, how to handle pretty basic differences of opinions, how to make phone calls when a stranger will be on the other end, and how to look someone in the eye and shake hands with new parents, teachers, or employers. We are also vastly underestimating the much deeper impact on our ability to love others. We are in the middle of making a silent, unintended sacrifice of our own thriving, growth, and purpose because we are increasingly refusing to interact with the crowd and get the much-needed practice of loving our neighbors.

To reap the benefits of crowds for a human soul, you need to (re)*learn how to be a neighbor*. To Jesus, the definition of *neighbor* was much broader than his Jewish contemporaries thought. He surprised people one day when he suggested that the idea of a "neighbor" stretched all the way into *the crowd*—a realm almost completely missing from Jewish life. This surprising interaction challenged people around him to consider the value of a stranger completely outside their notice. Jesus suggested that someone you pass by while living your life might contain a key to living deeper into the eternal, thriving life of God himself.

> On one occasion an expert in the law stood up to test Jesus. "Teacher," he asked, "**what must I do to inherit eternal life**?"
>
> "What is written in the Law?" he replied. "How do you read it?"
>
> He answered, "'Love the Lord your God with all your heart and with all your soul and with all your strength and with all your mind'; and, 'Love your neighbor as yourself.'"

"You have answered correctly," Jesus replied. "Do this and you will live."

But he wanted to justify himself, so he asked Jesus, "**And who is my neighbor?**" (Luke 10:25–29, emphasis added)

This second question "And who is my neighbor?" brought the real issue in this exchange to the surface. He was essentially asking Jesus, "Who am I obligated to love?" This man was looking for the answer to where to find true, eternal *life*, and Jesus knew what he'd been taught. The Jewish leaders of the day taught that the definition of *neighbor* (referenced from the Torah, Leviticus 19:18) was restricted to their *own Jewish community*. They put no emphasis or value on anyone outside of it. They'd essentially excluded the crowds around them. They knew the Scripture about loving your neighbor but had curated their lives to make that word mean a more palatable, manageable group of people. Over time, this hardened their hearts to any outsider deemed unclean, unworthy, and ungodly. Jesus pushed them to consider a new thought: What if you've missed the path to the life you want because of your definition of *neighbor*?

In reply Jesus said: "A man was going down from Jerusalem to Jericho, when he was attacked by robbers. They stripped him of his clothes, beat him and went away, leaving him half dead. A priest happened to be going down the same road, and when he saw the man, he passed by on the other side. So too, a Levite, when he came to the place and saw him, passed by on the other side. But a Samaritan, as he traveled, came where the man was; and when he saw him, he took pity on him. He went to him and bandaged his wounds, pouring on oil and wine. Then he put the man on his own donkey, brought him to an inn and took care of him. The next day he took out two denarii and gave them to the innkeeper. 'Look after him,' he said, 'and when I return, I will reimburse you for any extra expense you may have.' Which of these three do you think was a neighbor to the man who fell into the hands of robbers?" (Luke 10:30–36)

Jesus shockingly taught that the most law-abiding person in the story was a Samaritan, a categorical outsider to Jewish life and not even someone obligated to obey their law. Somehow the heart of the Samaritan had produced actions that better fulfilled the essence of God's law than the priest and Levite who tried to scrupulously obey it! Good Sam (as I call him) thought of "neighbor" as a *verb* instead of a noun. The Jewish leaders stayed "clean" by not dealing with blood and a potentially dead body. They avoided anything unpredictable or costly, not getting sidetracked on the way back to their own community. But in their devaluing of someone in the crowd, they were unable to find and live the life present within their own law. The key to the life of God lay in the engagement with the messy, unpredictable, unknown person on the side of the road. The stranger they passed by was an invitation to live the law as a verb instead of keeping it to themselves, protecting it as a noun. Jesus flipped the first question on its head and *neighbor* became not something you define but something you become.

> "Which of these three do you think was a neighbor to the man who fell into the hands of robbers?"
> The expert in the law replied, "**The one who had mercy on him.**" (Luke 10:36–37, emphasis added)

Your opportunities to live fully within the life of God require the crowds. Your willingness to love people beyond those you already know is essential for a life of purpose in the kingdom of God. Loving people you don't have to love is the clearest expression of the heart of a God who didn't *have to* love any of us. He chose to! He allowed himself to be sidetracked and inconvenienced out of the same thing that motivated the Samaritan: *compassion*. Compassion comes from the inside; obligation deals only with the outside. The priest and the Levite didn't see the chance to find life that day in the unexpected hiding place of God because they'd learned to think only of obligation, which hardened their hearts for compassion. "Who is my neighbor?" is a question asked by someone focused on external boundaries and obedience instead of internal, heart-level compassion. The sacrifice of Jesus was a mission of mercy, embodying the love of a compassionate God. We are invited into a life that furthers his purposes by doing the same.

The instinct of the experts in the law to limit the definition of *neighbor* is an understandable one to me. The call of the Law to "love your neighbor as yourself" feels huge and impossible—even crushing—if *everyone* is your neighbor. How is that really supposed to work? Most people I know already feel stretched thin, like we have barely enough to care adequately for our own core, circles, and comrades—let alone every single other person on the periphery of our life.

I was on an airplane a few weeks ago watching a mom try to manage three crying kids by herself. I had work to do. It would have been easy to join in with the exasperated looks she was getting and hope for the best. But, as a mom with four kids, I couldn't help but feel compassion when all she could do was watch as her kid two seats away kicked the guy next to him as she tried to calm the baby. I knew the stress and guilt and helplessness of knowing your kids were disturbing a lot of other people and everyone was judging you for it. It would have been easier to pass by on the other side. No one expected me to help. No one knew about my empathy. She certainly didn't expect me to help take care of them or show grace. It's moments like these we want to excuse ourselves, saying, "It's not my problem" or "She should have planned better." We tell ourselves we can't possibly be expected to be the answer of mercy for the thousands of people we pass by in a week. And that is true! Caring for thousands, hundreds, even scores of people we see in the crowd of our life each week is not realistic.

But one is.

The one right in front of you.

I didn't go looking for that mom, but there she was on my flight. The Good Samaritan didn't go seeking out strangers in the crowd, he simply found himself in front of one. The Samaritan was going about his normal life with a certain posture: *his eyes and his heart were open* to people he didn't know. He was willing to be the answer. I sometimes close my eyes or my heart for so many reasons. Sometimes I am overwhelmed at the need, and I tell myself I cannot help. I can be a crowd-avoider because I have a life that's already pretty full and I'm afraid I'll bite off more than I can chew. Sometimes I'm afraid I won't be received. For me, the truth is usually that I shrink back because I don't want to be interrupted from my predetermined plan. I protect myself and what I have going on in my own life. That was not the instinct of Good Sam. He saw the person in front of him and simply used the resources he had with him right then to address the very obvious need. He did it because he was the one who was there.

Our life only thrives if we risk being the answer and help in that moment. To be fully alive as a human soul, you need the challenge and the wonder buried in the act of loving strangers in a crowd. Expressing the *love* of God—to strangers, enemies, people who don't deserve your time and consideration in the crowd—ushers you into the *life* of God. What if you didn't worry about the external cost of saying yes but the internal cost of saying no? If I choose my protection or my safety or my community or my money or my schedule every time, I starve my soul. Jesus knows the life-giving, soul-thriving benefits of showing love and mercy to people who cannot return it. He loved you in a way you did not deserve and cannot return. He loved you when you were a stranger and an enemy of his Father in heaven. This is the unique opportunity waiting for you in the crowd: you get to practice loving like he did.

> **Expressing the *love* of God—to strangers, enemies, people who don't deserve your time and consideration in the crowd—ushers you into the *life* of God.**

> You see, at just the right time, when we were still powerless, Christ died for the ungodly. (Rom. 5:6)

Baylee was in the online crowd of my church. We have a very large online community made up of both people who attend in person and people who do not. I started to notice her name popping up time and again in online prayer services, in the comments section on Sundays, and in reactions to stories. Because it was during the Covid lockdowns, I was interacting online much more and noticed she had also started following my personal accounts, where I advertised a Bible study of Colossians. I didn't even know what city she lived in, but next thing I knew she was on my couch in a small group doing the study. Before the study ended, Baylee had a falling out with her roommate and needed a place to stay. Someone I'd only known a couple weeks was sitting right there in my living room and needed something. I felt compassion for her predicament, and pretty soon she was sleeping in my guest room and reading books to my daughter at bedtime. She went from online stranger to Bible study participant to guest room occupant in just a couple months.

I didn't have to offer her our empty room. Part of me didn't really want to because an extra person is bound to change the dynamics of a home. But there is a kind of life for your soul that only happens in showing care and compassion to someone in the crowd. My soul benefited from pushing through my "normal" way of life—one that always defaults to *me* in the center but leaves me frustrated that I can't seem to find more of the life I want. That life is hiding in the crowd. Your soul needs practice being a neighbor: wrestling through the questions and the sacrifice of *you* on behalf of someone else. God is always trying to grow and mature you, provide for you and others, and infuse your life with a sense of ongoing purpose and hope. Baylee just needed a place to land for a while, but God used her, someone from the crowd, to challenge our generosity, surrender our need for a plan, lay down our desire to be private with our home and family, and practice giving him access to all that we own on behalf of one of his other kids in need. He made us better neighbors, and it brought life to our souls.

Engaging the Crowd

Jesus was a great neighbor to the crowds because of his character, which is perfectly described in Exodus 34:6: "The LORD, the LORD, the compassionate and gracious God, slow to anger, abounding in love and faithfulness." This compassionate, good, gracious love of God is what moved Jesus to action many times and is what should move us into a crowd.

Crowds followed Jesus around as word got out about what he was doing. He gave healing, goodness, and help in abundance because he saw through the physical need of the person to the deeper need below it. His eyes were open to their spiritual condition, and it created in him a heart of compassion for strangers and outsiders of all kinds.

> Jesus went through all the towns and villages, teaching in their synagogues, proclaiming the good news of the kingdom and healing every disease and sickness. When he saw the crowds, he had compassion on them, because they were harassed and helpless, like sheep without a shepherd. (Matt. 9:35–36)

There are a few things you can do to engage the crowds in your life the way Jesus did. These leave you open and available but not crushed under the weight of taking on every burden or every person. Life-giving possibilities could be hiding in the crowd.

Watch for "The One"

Jesus watched and waited for *the one*: the one who stood out, the one in the crowd who was brave or desperate enough to come forward, the one who simply asked. In Mark 1:40 he healed a man with leprosy who came out of the crowd, begging for healing. In Mark 2 some friends of a paralyzed man dug a hole in the roof and lowered him down in front of Jesus. Jesus most often dealt with people in the crowd who caught his notice—like Zacchaeus. Zacchaeus, a corrupt tax collector, wanted to see Jesus, but he was too short to catch a glimpse above the crowd. So he climbed a tree. Jesus noticed the odd move. He stood out to Jesus, and by dinner Zacchaeus had repented of his past and entered a new life of faith. Jesus embraced the surprise and uncertainty of who would be *the one to come out of the crowd for more*. You have the freedom to wait for just the right one.

To love the crowds well in your life you have to cultivate awareness through the Holy Spirit *as you go*. Keep your eyes open for the unusual person, thought, or event. Watch for who comes toward you as you go about your day, work, travel, errands, or whatever. We are so used to walking through life with our heads down, looking at our phone, listening to our music, or feeling consumed by our own thoughts. What if you adopted a practice of keeping your phone in your purse or pocket at certain places—maybe the grocery line, the doctor's waiting room, or the bleachers at your kid's game? What if you set a reminder on your phone to go off at a certain location to remind you to pray? I am embarrassed to say that sometimes I simply forget that God thinks *the people around me* are the most important thing happening in any room. If you practice being more present wherever your two feet are, you'll find opportunities in the crowd.

You can have your "people radar" up anywhere—even in a restroom! I was washing my hands at a restaurant when a woman walked in. I noticed her very cool boots. I've learned to pay attention and respond to those tiny thoughts because they can be a gateway into a more significant exchange. So I said, "Hey, I love your boots. You look so good in them!" She turned around in surprise. She then confided in me that she felt women were too competitive about appearance and that it touched her heart I would compliment her so freely. I got the impression that my small comment had softened some bitterness she was holding on to, though I don't know for sure. What I do know is our exchange went deeper than the boots. When my husband tried to pay for our drinks twenty minutes later, the bartender pointed at her walking out ahead of us and said it was all taken care of. If I am paying attention, I can be a spontaneous part of what God is doing in the lives of the people around me in the crowd. I believe Jesus will review the impact of my life with me one day, and I'll learn how my interactions with others were a piece of something much larger he was up to. Maybe that will be the case for my little bathroom exchange, but, for now, I'm satisfied with the fact that we *both* left with a little more life in our souls that night.

> A person finds joy in giving an apt reply—
> and how good is a timely word! (Prov. 15:23)

Give without Expectation

I was surprised to realize that Jesus often did what we think of as his biggest and best miracles through one-off interactions in a crowd. He engaged generously even with strangers he'd never see again. When Jesus dealt with crowds, he wasn't closed off or selfish or stingy. He highlighted his practice of crowd generosity through the story of the Good Samaritan, who used his own money, oil, animal, and time to interact with a stranger. Sometimes you are the one equipped to help and sometimes you aren't. The first question when you see a need in the crowd is: "Do I have what is needed?" I know people—especially in a church setting—who overserve and try to meet every need, all the time, for everyone. You won't have the right stuff every time, but many times you will. The immediate next question to ask is: "Am I willing to give what I've got?" Sometimes the opportunity presented is more costly than we expect, and we simply aren't willing to sacrifice or risk our own resources.

I had a moment like this at a doctor's appointment. A wonderful nurse comforted me during a procedure. She was warm and clear and honest and made me smile. She was the best thing about a bad experience. As she prepped me, she remarked on my purse. (It is an *awesome* purse, made with beautiful leather and a couple of unusual design features.) I had gotten it as a gift, so we chatted about it, and I sang its praises. She asked for the brand, and we continued on with the appointment. As I was getting dressed, I had the fleeting thought I should buy her one—to encourage her, say thank you, and bless someone who was a light in a dark moment for me. I tried to blow it off, but the thought wouldn't go away. A few days later I found the purse online, and it cost *much* more than I expected. It made me both appreciate the generosity of the person who'd given it to me and simultaneously hesitate about buying one for the nurse. It was *way* more than I'd ever spent on a purse in my life.

I couldn't escape the thought that this idea had come from God, but I hesitated. Would God really ask me to be so extravagant? With a stranger? When I could easily blow off this idea and move on? So the first question I asked was, "Do I have the money to spend?" Yes. I had to shift something else, but I could definitely do it. For me the real question was, "Am I willing?" Am I willing to put my own money on the line to love someone in Jesus's name? When I don't have to? Will I risk it when I'm not absolutely sure?

Will I make a sacrifice somewhere else? I could easily have talked myself out of it because not all of me was completely willing. What won me over in the end was the extravagant love of Jesus.

Jesus valued the people in front of him *extravagantly*. Even those to whom society gave the least value—such as a little girl. He raised a young girl back to life after she had died. He also healed people with leprosy and women who'd been crippled. He asked tax collectors to host him for dinner or follow him as a disciple. Some of his most extravagant miracles were done to love people he could have justified not loving. Jesus gave lavishly because he saw their worth through the eyes of his Father. That's what won me over in the end: after a thumbs-up and a nudge from my unceasingly generous husband, I did buy what we now affectionately call "the nurse purse." The life it brought to my soul can't be measured. I could have stayed technically obedient to God by sticking to my tithe (giving 10 percent). I could have easily justified *not* giving this purse. But without it I couldn't have found the life that was waiting for me inside the command to be a good neighbor.

Don't Try to Take from a Crowd What You Can't Get

Crowds provide opportunities for each of us to practice loving as a neighbor loves, but they are not meant to provide other things—especially affirmation or approval for your identity or mission. It's tempting to chase that in a crowd, but they are a terrible source for what your core, circle, and comrades give—understanding, support, clarity, and affirmation of character and direction. If you go to a crowd for validation, it will backfire every time. You can't try to take from a crowd what they aren't meant to give. Jesus knew what people thought about him in their hearts and minds all the time, and there were always people around him misunderstanding his authority and actions.

> Jesus knew what they were thinking and asked, "Why are you thinking these things in your hearts? Which is easier: to say, 'Your sins are forgiven,' or to say, 'Get up and walk'?" (Luke 5:22–23)

The day Jesus said those words, he went on to heal a man in the crowd. His mission required crowd interaction, but he never looked to the bystanders for affirmation. Crowds are fickle. Jesus loved people in the crowds well because he was committed to his purpose, not because everyone standing around truly received him. When I interact with the crowds of my life, speaking to thousands, I have to be settled in my identity and my mission and know I am covered in grace. I already know they will not all approve. I have had people threaten me, insult me, call me names, and leave the church over me or something I said. If I need the approval of the crowds, I cannot do what God has given me to do.

Paul acknowledged the inherent tension between your mission and a crowd who is prone to misunderstand it, saying, "Am I now trying to win the approval of human beings, or of God? Or am I trying to please people? If I were still trying to please people, I would not be a servant of Christ" (Gal. 1:10). When we do not earn the approval of crowds it's awfully tempting to resort to trying to please them. The online crowds of social media offer a special temptation to people-please since the algorithms reward comments, activity, and more followers. It's easy to accidentally drift into pleasing the crowd instead of staying true to your mission. The crowd will eventually force you to make a choice to keep their approval.

The environment online encourages personal vulnerability and oversharing for the sake of growing an audience, so we tend to treat crowds as closer friends than they are. This is the biggest mistake we make in this realm of relationship: The crowd should not be given the same information about you as your core. They shouldn't be given the same access to you as your circle. You shouldn't mistake them for comrades on your mission or even a community that is in your corner. A crowd cannot be trusted to reliably provide any of those things. Don't look to the crowd for what they aren't equipped to offer you.

Take Time Away

We have to stay clearheaded about what a crowd is and isn't and also limit the amount of time we spend in that space. Crowds require our regular withdrawal. They can be disorienting and all-consuming with so many needs, opinions, and directions. The more crowds gathered in the life of Jesus, the more regularly he withdrew from them: "Yet the news about him spread all the more, so that crowds of people came to hear him and to be healed of their sicknesses. But Jesus often withdrew to lonely places and prayed" (Luke 5:15–16).

Only God can help you clarify your interactions in the crowd. Hit the reset button and draw back into prayer if you can't explain things like why you're posting on social media the way you are or why you can't be alone or why you get crushed in spirit without everyone's approval. You do *not* have to engage everyone you meet. Sometimes Jesus walked away from the crowds to be with his circle or to be alone with his Father. Sometimes he walked away from crowds because they were draining, hostile, or it simply wasn't the right time. Relationally healthy people have regular times of withdrawal from the crowd, such as times without social media interaction, spaces and places where they are alone, patterns of prayer, and good boundaries around what they will and will not share in various relational spaces. Crowds can take from you in a unique way, but, with the right mindset, they can also bring a unique kind of life and fulfillment to your soul.

Crowd Loneliness

For nearly seven years I missed a lot of that fulfillment because crowds were virtually nonexistent in my life. I had four babies age five and under. I knew I was loved in all my other relationships, but I just felt a little off in a way I couldn't quite put my finger on. I know now it was the loneliness of a missing crowd. My days seemed flat and devoid of excitement even when they were full of tasks and necessary activities. Sometimes I'd go to the park to see if other moms might be around, hoping maybe God would bring something interesting to change up the routine of naps and feedings and preschool pickups. I could look at the days ahead and tell you every single face I was going to see for weeks on end, and I could count them on less than two hands.

I was absolutely starved for something I didn't even know was missing. My soul was hurting. I told myself I was being ungrateful. I told myself I should be content with the things around me. I repeatedly tried to talk myself out of this loneliness, but the truth is that we are made for some kind of interaction with crowds that helps us feel fully alive. I shamed myself for wanting to offer something to someone that wasn't the milk in my breasts. I wish I'd known there is a part of our soul that can only be fulfilled in unwritten exchanges with the crowd. I would have understood what I felt a bit better. Fresh interactions bring fresh possibilities, so crowds help us live expectantly.

There is a kind of thriving that comes with a sense that you can make an unpredictable impact on someone's day everywhere you are, every day you are alive. If you interact well in the crowds of your life, there is a specific sense of loneliness that you keep at bay. This kind of loneliness feels a lot like boredom or weariness. For me it carried a sense of guilt because the other realms all seem more important. Whether they are or aren't, crowds do offer something unique that will leave a little hole in the fabric of your soul when it's missing. It's a loneliness that diminishes your sense of vibrancy and *hope*. You are made to wake up every day feeling expectant of what God may do with the hours in front of you. God made you to walk through life with him and encounter unplanned ways to help or bless or love someone around you.

Crowds not only add potential for us to be hopeful for more but also for us to grow more certain of God's presence everywhere we go. Most of us never catch the glimpse that is buried inside the crowd of the invisible, incredible potential for God to show up in our lives. I think I catch more glimpses than the average person because of my job. A couple years ago at an Ohio State basketball game I was walking back into the arena with a drink and had forgotten to look at my section number. The usher took one look at me and said "Hi, Alli!" I was two hours from home with twenty thousand people in a basketball arena and someone knew me. She had watched my sermons online and followed our church. I instantly felt a sense of belonging in the huge crowd at the Schottenstein Center. Not only did she help me back to my seat, but we exchanged social media follows and a hug. I've had other people pay for my meal or talk to me as I get coffee at Panera. I've even had a couple stop me on a cruise ship in the middle of the ocean to say, "Hey! We go to Crossroads! Great to see you!" This is the good part of being recognizable at a very large church—people come out of the crowd to say hey, and I get to see the proof that *God's people really are everywhere!* We all struggle with the thought that we are alone, but that is never true. It's as if I've been given a pair of glasses that let me see through the crowds of strangers to realize that there is a God who has access to me *through his people* anytime he wants. And these are just the ones from my own church! Just imagine how many followers of Jesus there are anywhere you go. Even in the moments you feel alone, the truth is in Psalm 139:7–12:

> Where can I go from your Spirit?
>> Where can I flee from your presence?
> If I go up to the heavens, you are there;
>> if I make my bed in the depths, you are there.
> If I rise on the wings of the dawn,
>> if I settle on the far side of the sea,
> even there your hand will guide me,
>> your right hand will hold me fast.
> If I say, "Surely the darkness will hide me
>> and the light become night around me,"
> even the darkness will not be dark to you;
>> the night will shine like the day,
>> for darkness is as light to you.

God is present through the Spirit in his people. He can send one to the far side of the sea for you if needed. Or send you to them. He can light up any darkness, and there is no place you will ever go that God cannot reach you. And you get to be part of reaching someone else in the same way! We all desperately need to know that God is all around us. He has people in every crowd; you are never alone.

Your Crowd Holds Divine Appointments

I call them *divine appointments*, but that's just my term for it. These are the seemingly random intercepts that God arranges in the crowd. I believe God uses crowds as a place he can cross the paths of two people who may not ever otherwise meet. He can do it for *any* kind of purpose, so crowds can be ripe with interactions led by his Spirit. I have walked into many crowded rooms and quietly said to God, "Show me what you're doing here. Who do you want me to talk to?" because I believe he may even send *me* into some situations to be a divine appointment for another person. I used to stand in the huge atrium on the second level of our church, looking down as people poured in on a Sunday morning, and ask God to point out someone I should go meet in the crowd. I met a young mom this way when I heard the Spirit "whisper" a thought to me: *Don't walk away without getting her phone number*. It's twelve years later and she's now part of my core.

Mary and Joseph took Jesus into a big crowd at the temple after he was born, and God led them straight to a couple strangers who almost seemed to be expecting them. Mary and Joseph were there to have Jesus dedicated after his birth at the standard time, according to the Jewish law for the consecration of firstborn sons, but God used it as a moment to confirm his Son's identity and prophesy about his life. He had arranged for two people to be there. Jesus's parents experienced two divine appointments waiting for them in the crowd, and Luke records that they "marveled" at what took place there when they encountered Simeon and Anna.

The first was Simeon: "Now there was a man in Jerusalem called Simeon, who was righteous and devout. He was waiting for the consolation of Israel, and the Holy Spirit was on him. It had been revealed to him by the Holy Spirit that he would not die before he had seen the Lord's Messiah. **Moved by the Spirit, he went into the temple courts.** When the parents brought in the child Jesus to do for him what the custom of the Law required, Simeon took him in his arms and praised God" (Luke 2:25–28, emphasis added).

The second divine appointment for Mary and Joseph was with Anna: "There was also a prophet, Anna, the daughter of Penuel, of the tribe of Asher. . . . She never left the temple but worshiped night and day, fasting and praying. **Coming up to them at that very moment**, she gave thanks to God and spoke about the child to all who were looking forward to the redemption of Jerusalem" (Luke 2:36–38, emphasis added).

The Spirit of God can move people into crowds wherever we are at any moment. God set me up to intersect someone in a crowd in August 2003. If you don't live in the Northeastern United States or Ontario, you might not remember a massive regional blackout that happened that month. It was the worst regional power blackout in the history of either the United States or Canada, and a lot of people outside the region never even paid attention. I sure did because my plane landed in New York City thirty minutes after the power went out. No one knew the scale of what had just happened. Technically I landed at Newark airport, which is just across from Manhattan in New Jersey. So I waited eight hours in a cab line (no Ubers back then!) only to find out that all the bridges and tunnels into the city were closed as a precaution in the chaos that was ensuing. The city was where my hotel room was ready for me. It's also where my brother's apartment was. My phone didn't work because all the networks were down. People began to grasp the scale of the blackout just as it got dark and panic set in.

I made it to a nearby hotel where, because the keys weren't working, the security systems were down. They couldn't check in any new guests and were verifying identities, escorting guests one by one to their rooms, and letting them in with one master key. In protection for their current guests, they announced at eleven o'clock that anyone without a room key was going to be tossed off the property at midnight. I went to the bar, ordered a drink, and cried. And prayed. I, a young woman in my twenties, was alone in the city, about to be put out on the streets where people were looting and everything was in pitch darkness. I begged a security guard to let me stay. He told me he'd do his best to keep an eye on me during his rounds if I stayed near the property entrance. I was terrified, but I told myself it was better than nothing.

At 11:55 p.m. I got a tap on the shoulder. A man from a group of Wells Fargo employees sitting nearby was holding out a room key.

I just stared at it. I thought for a moment he was going to ask me if I wanted to share his room. He must have sensed my hesitation because he said, "Don't you need a room? You can have this one. It was my coworker's, and she found a rental car to drive home." I felt saved by God himself! This was a surreal, eleventh-hour rescue. Looking back, it was definitely a divine appointment. I just happened to pick the table right next to the one person there with an extra key, and he offered it to me with literally five minutes to spare.

The next day I woke up and realized I was in the Wells Fargo employees' block of rooms. They had their doors propped open and were trying to figure out how to get home. News had spread about the blackout, and no phones were working, no airports in the area were operational, and there were no rental cars left anywhere. But they'd somehow found themselves an expensive car service to get to Baltimore. They'd somehow gotten one cell phone to work briefly and the one call that magically got through was to their travel agents while I was standing there talking with them.

They said, "Hey, do you want us to get you a ticket home?" I stared at them blankly. "Where's home?" they asked. "Let us buy you a ticket." And the next thing I knew I was squashed between five Wells Fargo guys on a long drive to Baltimore with a plane ticket home to Cincinnati. I didn't pay a cent. Someone from the crowd saved me not once but twice, by the grace of God. I knew this was God's utterly miraculous provision through a divine appointment with these men in the crowd who kept me safe and got me home. I never saw them again. God can do amazing things with people buried in the crowd.

You are never alone.

Where Are Your Crowds?

Write the names of your crowds in the margins around this blueprint.

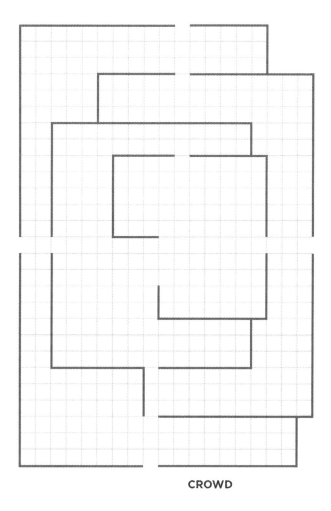

CROWD

First, jot down the places where you go on a regular basis. Where are you around strangers? Do you encounter crowds at the mall, a campus, the gym, an office building, the airport, etc.?

Write down places you find yourself waiting/standing/ killing time the most. The pharmacy line? Kids' activities? Before/after meetings? During lunch in a cafeteria?

Where do you encounter crowds online?

Now look back over your original attempt to list out *all* your relationships (pp. 36–37). Are there any people who are unaccounted for? Are any of these names basically just strangers—or very nearly so—who belong in your crowd? Put them on the blueprint too.

Is there a small habit you could adopt that would make you more present to the people around you? Choose one of the places above and memorize this prayer of mine adapted from Ephesians 1:18–19 to pray every time you walk in the door:

Lord, let me see into this crowd with your eyes so I can fulfill your call on my life to offer the riches of your hope and power to others. Amen.

Now that you've worked through all the realms of relationship in the life of Jesus, let's consider one last kind of relationship: **counterfeits**. Counterfeits are people in your life who appear to belong with you but, upon closer inspection, are just imitating one of these five authentic relationships . . . and their impact on your soul can be destructive.

The Cost of Counterfeits

I urge you, brothers and sisters, to watch out for those who cause divisions and put obstacles in your way that are contrary to the teaching you have learned. Keep away from them.

Romans 16:17

About a year ago I walked away from a relationship in my life. I had long since wrestled with the frustrating nature of our connection. I felt guilty for not wholeheartedly maintaining it and forced myself to keep it going. I secretly blamed myself because of my lack of desire to connect. I got to the point where pretty much everything I did was out of obligation. I finally admitted to myself the truth I'd known deep down: the relationship was lifeless. The hallmark of a counterfeit relationship? It never brings life to your soul. There are so many reasons why relationships become strained or difficult. Many of those reasons are worthy of reconciliation, repentance, and repair. And some are not. This particular bond was a relic of some relationship "rules" I'd soaked in growing up. No one ever said it directly, but I picked up the idea that there were some people you were just *required* to maintain a relationship with at any cost. Why? Because it kept up appearances on the outside.

You likely have at least one relationship that isn't just difficult but, rather, **counterfeit**. From the outside they may look like someone who should be in your core, circle, comrades, or community, but the bond never produces real thriving in that space. These types of relationships are disorienting: from the outside they look good. We tend to let these hollow connections linger because we probably keep thinking it's going to work, or it should work, or it used to work. If you're anything like me, sometimes you just aren't ready to pay the cost of walking away. The thought of cutting relationships out of our lives can bring up deep fears around losing the very sense of belonging we're trying to build, or the fear of being alone. So we keep counterfeits inside the blueprints of our relational world and try to be satisfied with something that at least *looks* like the real thing. But if you maintain empty attachments indefinitely, the condition of your soul will suffer: there's a cost to counterfeits.

After conversations I'd find myself thinking, "Why is this always so draining? Why can't I enjoy this person? Why do I make myself do this?" I finally talked it over with my husband and a trusted friend, who both agreed: for years they hadn't seen any fruit. This dutiful attachment was masquerading as something meaningful. When I finally stopped, it was both an internal and external process. I had to forgive myself for breaking the "rules" of being nice and maintaining this relationship because I was "supposed to." I also had to give up the habits of phone calls and required get-togethers that had maintained this connection. It was hard. It's been many months now since we've spoken. Saying I feel *good* about it would go too far, but I'm relieved not to carry the dissonance of years of tending and watering with no fruit.

Counterfeits Look Like the Real Thing

The hallmark of counterfeit relationships is that, at first glance, they look like the real thing. It's entirely possible not to know at first—or just to miss the signs as you welcome someone into any part of your relational world. All your people take up space inside your mind and heart. For the life of your soul, those connections need to produce vitality in your inner being. Otherwise, you're just carrying dead weight in your community, comrades, or circle. I name those three types of relationships specifically because it is unlikely for someone to make it into the innermost core of your life without a genuinely life-giving connection, and your crowd is full of people you don't know yet. So the potential to discover counterfeit connections is mostly within your community, comrades, or circle. Jesus dealt with counterfeit relationships in these places too. From the very first days of his ministry, he had to decide how to deal with relationships that feigned the real thing.

Jesus found counterfeits within his community of religious leaders in Israel, specifically the group called the Pharisees. It looked like a place for Jesus to have genuine connection. On the surface there was a shared passion for the law and many theological foundations in common—the most out of any subgroup of religious leaders in Israel. They should have made great comrades in religious scholarship and in their common desire to lead Israel closer to God. But the Pharisees showed evidence over and over that their hearts were far from God. Their actions revealed completely different motives than the ones Jesus had. Over time, a few Pharisees wanted to authentically connect with Jesus, but the vast majority fell into the category of counterfeit relationships. They weren't really interested in Jesus; they only cared about how he impacted their own agenda. Their hearts—and therefore their eyes—could not truly see what God was doing because they were so focused on themselves. This selfishness created mixed motives and conflict with Jesus, who pointed out their inconsistencies: "Woe to you, teachers of the law and Pharisees, you hypocrites! You shut the door of the kingdom of heaven in people's faces" (Matt. 23:13).

John the Baptist also used a term for the Pharisees that hints at this disconnect between their inside and outside: he called the Pharisees a "brood of vipers" (Matt. 3:7). Vipers were thought to be beautiful on the outside even as they have venom on the inside. They look good, but they *take* life. The Pharisees loved wearing the right clothes and enjoying the honor of leadership, but their hearts were far from God. They had no inner life, but the shiny surface fooled people who came looking to find the life of God in connection with them.

This same thing might mark a counterfeit in your life: the relationship looks great from the outside, but you privately know there is nothing of quality or substance below the surface. Jesus sensed empty, false motives and cleverly protected himself from their impact. He instructed his own disciples, warning them like he did in Matthew 16:11–12: "'Be on your guard against the yeast of the Pharisees and Sadducees.' Then they understood that he was not telling them to guard against the yeast used in bread, but against the teaching of the Pharisees and Sadducees." Jesus put the Pharisees in a different relational category altogether. If you read about his treatment of them over time, you can see that Jesus stayed away from them when he could and pushed back strongly on their falsehoods when the welfare of others was at stake. It can take a while to see a mismatch between the outside and the inside of someone's life—and then redirect your path.

I wish I'd given myself permission earlier in life to even recognize this kind of relationship existed, but I didn't. So I missed the signs as early as high school. There was a guy in my high school geometry class who was funny and charming, and I really liked sitting next to him in class. All year I thought we made a real, fun connection; I honestly considered us friends. One day he came looking for me in a crowded hallway, yelling, "Al! Al! Where are you?" Only my two brothers have ever called me Al, so I came around the lockers with a smile on my face. I certainly did not expect the demanding words "Give me your homework." When I wouldn't let him cheat off me, he got mad. Really mad. He told me he only sat by me in class so he could copy my answers and he did it all the time. He tried to convince me that the only difference now was because I knew about it. As he yelled "Please, Al, c'mon . . . please. I don't know why you're so mad," I walked away feeling the disorienting impact of a counterfeit connection.

Counterfeits Want a Payoff

It was the classic sign of a counterfeit connection: the question looming over these relationships is, "What's in it for me?" Jesus saw this same focus on personal gain in his interactions with the Pharisees. Counterfeit connection happens if one person (or both of you) values what they get out of the relationship more than what they put in. Maybe you keep up a relationship because it means you also get your parents' approval or it connects you to a group you want to be in. Do you stay in touch with someone because you want to have a place to stay in that city? Do you keep them in your life because they own a business and give you a discount? Sometimes it's as blatant as being used by someone for your homework, but most of the time it's the much more subtle gains of image, security, reputation, or self-worth. The heart can harbor very quiet motives to seek friendship for something beyond the actual bond itself. God warned his people of their tendency to drift this direction through the words of Jeremiah: "The heart is deceitful above all things and beyond cure. Who can understand it?" (17:9).

This is why it's healthy to check your own motives for maintaining the connections you have. For most of us—if we are honest with ourselves—we have mixed motives in some relationships. I confess I have found myself desiring a connection with someone but being far more interested in gaining access to their professional network than connecting with their heart. I'm not proud of that, but the motives inside our own hearts need to be examined and constantly renewed in a world that encourages us to go get what's ours—to put external benefit first in relationships.

I have a friend who owns a few of the best restaurants in our region of the country, and they're often filled with celebrities and high-profile events. She needs to maintain relationships that exist in an odd gray area between true friendship and mutual gain. She has had to develop a Spirit-led radar for seeing the differences between friends, business associates, and patently false connections in an environment where people have lots of reasons for wanting to connect with her or her business. Many of us have been hurt by someone who only wanted us around when we were good for them or helped their image or advanced their work. My sweet daughter just told me about a girl at school who won't say hello to her around the cool girls but wants to hang with her at recess because my daughter's team always wins at kickball. As we get older we just develop more sophisticated ways of winning the games we are playing.

In Matthew 6, Jesus detailed some of the practices of people just looking for a payoff. His words were for those who approach a relationship to God that way—only for what they can get *out* of it. He wanted his followers to recognize real versus counterfeit ties in others—and in themselves. The same principles are true for our human bonds as well: in every instance, the counterfeit version is motivated by external reward.

- "So when you give to the needy, do not announce it with trumpets, as the hypocrites do in the synagogues and on the streets, to be honored by others. Truly I tell you, they have received their reward in full" (v. 2).
- "And when you pray, do not be like the hypocrites, for they love to pray standing in the synagogues

and on the street corners to be seen by others. Truly I tell you, they have received their reward in full" (v. 5).

- "When you fast, do not look somber as the hypocrites do, for they disfigure their faces to show others they are fasting. Truly I tell you, they have received their reward in full" (v. 16).

The core motivation of all these behaviors was image, honor, and reputation. Jesus calls them out as hypocrites. Ouch. But that's what counterfeit relationships turn us into if we hold on to them long enough. They become a place for an exchange of benefits, a performance of connection while insisting "it's not about that." The things being done by the hypocrites Jesus spoke to—giving, praying, fasting—were supposedly being done to strengthen their relationship with God. But in reality, these activities were only a way to win the prizes of image and reputation. The payoff was what they wanted. Even "good" spiritual activities done with that motive can hold zero benefit for connecting with God. The same is true for ulterior motives when connecting with friends.

Any friendship for gain will always leave a gnawing sense of loneliness in your soul because no real connection is taking place. Jesus underscored this as he repeated the sentence, "Truly I tell you, they have received their reward in full." The immediate, external payoff is all it will ever yield. The benefits of counterfeit relationships may in fact be real, but they quickly vanish and leave an empty space behind. The best bonds, with God and others, have a payoff of expanding life and hope. Our souls become anchored in a belief that the best is always yet to come. The more we give away space in our blueprint to counterfeit connections, the greater the cost to our soul.

Counterfeits Are Costly

I pay a cost to meet with a few women every other week on Friday mornings. Sometimes as I park I think about the work I could be getting done or the workout I need to get into my day or the fact that they will ask why I'm grumpy or down when I don't feel like talking. All relationships cost something to keep. They cost us in time, emotional capacity, money for gas or coffee, or just the focus we could put on other things. However, every week when I walk out the door, I feel silly for thinking the cost might not be worth it. I am filled up by these connections with life I can't get any other way. I am full of more faith in God and more love for others. I am filled inside by support and wisdom, and I feel less alone. The cost is *always* worth receiving that kind of life. If you sustain empty relationships, you will still pay the external costs—but with no nourishment for your soul. Only in true life-giving attachments are souls revived.

In counterfeit connections there is external cost without internal replenishment. Soul-filling can only be found in the kinds of relationships that aren't trying to take something from us. This mirrors the love of God, which your soul was literally made for—a love that doesn't require something in return, one that's always out for your good. Whether it's the unconditional commitment from your core or a simple, onetime interaction in the crowd, you only receive life when connections are free from the requirement of reciprocation.

Jesus knew how much our souls need the nutrition of authentic connection with God and others to survive. He not only refused to keep up relationships with a hollow core in his own life, but he pushed back *hard* on any depiction of a relationship with God as a system of external reward. In Luke 11 he stood firm against the Pharisees' rules that brought no internal life. They questioned him about why he didn't follow certain regulations, and he responded with a stern word about their obsession with external requirements over the internal life of their soul:

> Now then, you Pharisees clean the outside of the cup and dish, but inside you are full of greed and wickedness. You foolish people! Did not the one who made the outside make the inside also? But now as for what is inside you—be generous to the poor, and everything will be clean for you. (Luke 11:39–41)

Jesus said their hyperfocus on "paying" external costs to be clean (i.e., to find life) was actually keeping them from it! Jesus confused and convicted them by suggesting the law could only be fulfilled when one had a clean heart and no sneaky motives for gain. His example—generosity to the poor—is the antithesis of a counterfeit act of love. The poor could give nothing in return, so they were of course regularly overlooked by the Pharisees, who knew only counterfeit connections. Jesus issued a strong warning against the what's-in-it-for-me mentality as one wholly incompatible with *love*. If love is the motivation of the heart, loving someone will ultimately come at a personal cost that counterfeit relationships aren't willing to pay. And it won't end well.

Counterfeit Connections End Badly

The counterfeit relationship in Jesus's circle—his relationship with Judas—ended very badly. In the end it came down to a choice: Jesus or personal gain? If you have ever had a "friend" you're pretty sure would throw you under the bus for something they really wanted, then you know who Judas was. Jesus knew the pain of having a counterfeit connection revealed in your closest circle of friends. The closer the friend, the deeper the betrayal.

There had been glimpses all along of what Judas wanted the most. It was *money*. Money had competed for his affections and loyalties for a long time. People around him saw small moments of this hidden agenda at work, like the day a woman showed up with an extravagant gift for Jesus in gratitude for their relationship. The beauty of real connection was lost on Judas, so he grumbled a false objection out of his hidden motive.

> But one of his disciples, Judas Iscariot, who was later to betray him, objected, "Why wasn't this perfume sold and the money given to the poor? It was worth a year's wages." He did not say this because he cared about the poor but because he was a thief; as keeper of the money bag, he used to help himself to what was put into it. (John 12:4–6)

Jesus warned that this same counterfeit agenda was at work in the heart of the Pharisees, and they eventually teamed up with Judas to bring Jesus down, perfectly fulfilling the truth Jesus had once taught them.

> "No one can serve two masters. Either you will hate the one and love the other, or you will be devoted to the one and

despise the other. You cannot serve both God and money."
The Pharisees, who loved money, heard all this and were
sneering at Jesus. (Luke 16:13–14)

As you're considering whether some connections in your
life are counterfeit, it's great to ask yourself, "Who is this
person really serving?" Judas had a slow drift away from God
until the night he took thirty pieces of silver from the Pharisees to betray his friend's location for his final arrest. Judas's
love of money turned this relationship into a counterfeit that
took Jesus to the cross. For several years their connection
simply grew alongside the other apostles, the false nature
only rearing its head in small glimpses, until the seeds of
money grew enough to choke out anything fruitful inside
Judas. It took several years to be able to see that Judas was
a false apostle, and Jesus allowed him to keep growing in his
circle until his heart became fully visible in his final betrayal.

Counterfeit Connections Are Seen in the Fruit

Like with Judas, false associations eventually show themselves,
even if they were under the surface for a long time. Don't be
afraid to change your mind or admit there was something you
didn't initially see. I always want to see the best in people, so
it can be hard to let myself acknowledge this. I choose instead
to blame myself for being critical or not having enough love
and patience to bear with someone's faults. (Which has occasionally been the case.) But despite my own shortcomings,
time will always bring the counterfeit nature of a relationship
to the surface in an undeniable way. It can be really hard to
admit when something needs to end, so Jesus prescribed a
clear method for us: *look at the fruit*. Relationships bear fruit

you can see. Jesus told a parable in Matthew 13 acknowledging the difficulty sometimes in telling the difference between something that is growing and will satisfy your soul and something that won't. It's called the parable of the sower.

In the parable, seed from the enemy of God (weeds) grows alongside good seed (wheat). In the region of Israel where Jesus lived, the two plants he referenced in this parable were so similar that it was nearly impossible to distinguish between them until harvest time. At harvest time you can see the fruit. That's the moment to decide what the plants were all along. Just as Judas fit in with all the other disciples for so long, there was a point when the fruit of his heart and their relationship became clear. Jesus finished his parable with these words: "Let both grow together until the harvest. At that time I will tell the harvesters: First collect the weeds and tie them in bundles to be burned; then gather the wheat and bring it into my barn" (Matt. 13:30). When you suspect a relationship is counterfeit, the next question has to be, "Is now the right time to decide?" Sometimes you need to wait and see the fruit. But once you do see it, wheat always stays wheat and weeds stay weeds. The relationships to invest in are the ones that nourish life for both of you from the inside out.

Jesus was big on the "look for the fruit" method of evaluation. He knew our propensity for both self-deception and judgment. Our eyes aren't always clear. Our hearts don't always lead us with the right motives. Sometimes you desperately want to find the good in keeping a connection with someone. Sometimes you get fooled by a great outward show of leaves and beauty. But the fruit never lies. In the end, this was Jesus's conclusion about the Pharisees: there was *just no fruit*. None in their hearts. None in their leadership. None in their nation. None in their faith. Early in his ministry, Jesus had issued this warning to the people:

> Watch out for false prophets. They come to you in sheep's clothing, but inwardly they are ferocious wolves. By their fruit you will recognize them. Do people pick grapes from thornbushes, or figs from thistles? Likewise, every good tree bears good fruit, but a bad tree bears bad fruit. A good tree cannot bear bad fruit, and a bad tree cannot bear good fruit. Every tree that does not bear good fruit is cut down and thrown into the fire. Thus, by their fruit you will recognize them. (Matt. 7:15–20)

He literally said to watch for the fruit and you'll know what's real. The religious leaders never understood what Jesus meant. They didn't know that the good stuff grows from the inside out—never the outside in. So, in the end, Jesus told the Pharisees, "Therefore I tell you that the kingdom of God will be taken away from you and given to a people who will produce its fruit" (Matt. 21:43). He repeatedly encouraged us to be clear-eyed in search of real fruit in relationships with both God and others. Fruit is the visible outcome of what has been growing all along. Fruit is what is given to us by God for both life and pleasure, from things that are alive and healthy. The same is true in your relational world. God used the imagery of fruit in Scripture from the very beginning of Genesis, through the Prophets, in the New Testament letters, all the way to the very end of Revelation, to indicate places that were good, growing, and able to sustain your life.

Look for the fruit. And believe your own eyes.

As you begin the tough exercise of considering where you might be keeping up counterfeit connections, first check your own heart with this prayer that starts from Luke 18:13. This could only come from a heart able to bear good fruit:

> God, *have mercy on me, a sinner.*
> *I confess my heart has mixed motives.*
> *I know my eyes cannot fully see the people around me.*
> *Help me discern, by your Spirit, any relationships that aren't going to bear fruit.*
> *Show me whether now is the time to separate from them. Amen.*

Quick note to you married people: Sometimes marriages are hurting. Believe me, I get it. This chapter is not meant to address your spouse. Once you are married, God sees you as one, so the relationship is in a category of its own, deserving much more consideration than any other human connection. If this chapter made you think of your marriage in any way, I encourage you to seek the depth of love and support you need to explore that far beyond the pages of this book, with peer, pastoral, and counseling help in the spirit of full reconciliation.

Now, consider any names from the beginning of the book that you never wrote down in any other part of your blueprint. Do any of them belong here? Write down those names you want to consider further:

Now, think about these relationships by answering these questions in search of fruitfulness:

- What are the good things that have come from this connection?
- How has it nourished you on the inside?
- Is there new growth in your life you associate with this bond?
- Is there a benefit to your reputation or self-image?
- Is there an external benefit you receive from this person?
- Has your perspective on this relationship changed over time at all?
- What would be missing from your life if this association dissolved?

Pray this prayer from Psalm 139:23–24:

Search me, God, and know my heart;
    test me and know my anxious thoughts.
See if there is any offensive way in me,
    and lead me in the way everlasting.

The Center of Christ

Indeed, the water I give them will become in them a spring of water welling up to eternal life.

John 4:14

Human souls are designed for these five types of relationships, but the reality of our lives is much messier than simply finding and snapping five puzzle pieces together. The longer I live, the more aware I've become that my relationships are constantly changing. The latest shift always seems to result in some sort of new deficiency in or interruption to the connection and belonging I desire with other people. I remember an especially hard adjustment in my twenties when I came out of college. My core people were suddenly scattered across the country, and I had no circle in a brand-new city, so I threw myself into my new career. I tried to meet all my needs in one place and with one set of people—my brand-new set of coworkers. I now realize the pressure I put on these new relationships to fulfill needs in parts of my blueprint they were not yet cultivated to fulfill. Perhaps they could have been solid community—maybe even a few comrades—but I tried to squeeze them all into my smaller, closer spaces where they didn't yet fit. I badly needed the unconditional commitment of a core to support all this change. I yearned to be included in a circle, as I had been the previous four years. I tried to use my performance at work to earn approval and to secure the sense of belonging that my postcollege world sorely lacked.

I was missing a strong and constant sense of belonging that wasn't dependent on the shifts of my relationships. My inner life needed an unchanging, life-giving presence in the center. As created, embodied souls, we are made for this type of connection with God himself. When you are filled with him in the very deepest places, life flows from the middle, outward into all your other connections—even into the empty spots that are created during the constant transitions of our lives. When the right mix of people is missing for a while, your bond with God will keep you standing when holes appear. It also ensures that even your strongest relationships function the way they should. When my connection with God is weak or not in place, I will inevitably try to use human relationships to fill voids they weren't meant to fill, damaging even the best of bonds.

I definitely did that. My quest for approval, worth, and acknowledgment in my twenties almost ruined my marriage. I bent myself around whatever it took to be seen and included by the people I respected, and to feel as if I had important work (which are all things God would have loved to provide to me first). The good relationship I *did* have was almost ruined by what I *didn't* have in the center of my life: a real connection with God. I allowed my job to dictate everything else about my life. I was selfish with my husband about where we lived. I wanted approval from bosses above him or even occasionally against my own better judgment. I worked hours that hurt my brand-new marriage. I competed with coworkers for attention at work instead of seeking my husband's attention above anyone else. I was yearning for something in the center that was missing. And all of this happened *after* I'd believed in Jesus! The right theological or intellectual belief about God isn't enough to fill these voids. Morality isn't enough. Going to church isn't enough. This hole at the center wreaked havoc because I wasn't yet fostering a connection with the Spirit of Christ in the very middle of my life and being. So I went looking inside my other relationships for what only he can give.

I forgive myself for what I didn't see then. I simply did not know there is a living Source that can flow from the center into everything else. I've learned this through the life of Jesus and lots of experiments to trust him. Jesus lived with a constant and primary connection to the Father, and therefore flourished in his human connections as a result. There has only ever been one perfectly functioning, perfectly fulfilled, and completely alive human soul (and it isn't me!). It was the man we call Jesus Christ. Jesus had no rips, tears, or holes that he tried to plug with his human relationships. He lived in deep connection with his Father, so his relational world, inasmuch as it depended on him, worked exactly as it was designed.

Blueprint for Belonging

Life from the Source

Jesus lived fully alive on the inside in a way we probably cannot ever accurately grasp. I recently woke up one morning to my own internal condemning thoughts about drinking an extra glass of wine the night before. I then zoned out listening to one of my kids talk on our drive to school, accidentally hurting her feelings. (In my defense it was a really long explanation of something very inconsequential that happened in chorus class the previous day.) Before it even hit two o'clock in the afternoon, I'd also received a nicely worded text from a colleague who said I was insensitive to someone's feelings when I'd actually thought I was being helpful. And that all happened on a *good* day!

The impact of sin on the inside and outside of our lives is so great that none of us have any concept of what it would feel like to live without having to battle such messed up thoughts or illegitimate desires, without occasionally saying stupid things to the people around you, or without your internal "bad place" (where you spiral down a dark hole, convinced you are unloved or rejected or afraid or alone). The inner life of Jesus somehow worked very differently than ours. There was no disconnection due to sin or his own brokenness, so he was free to live in seamless connection with his Father. Jesus spoke of a Source that overwhelms with *life* from the inside out.

The Gospels testify to this connection with the Source from the very beginning of Jesus's time on earth, beginning in the womb, just as the angel explained to Mary. "The Holy Spirit will come on you, and the power of the Most High will overshadow you. So the holy one to be born will be called the Son of God" (Luke 1:35). Another glimpse of his

182

awareness and passion for their bond took place when Jesus was a boy. His family couldn't find him, and he turned up in the temple courts, sitting among the teachers, who were amazed at his insight. They couldn't explain it any other way at his young age: "Everyone who heard him was amazed at his understanding and his answers" (Luke 2:47). Jesus knew exactly where his learning came from. When Mary and Joseph questioned him on his whereabouts for the prior three days, he answered, "Didn't you know I had to be in my Father's house?" (Luke 2:49).

Years later, in the beginning of his earthly ministry, Jesus received a public heavenly acknowledgment of this loving connection when his Father spoke in a voice from heaven, saying, "You are my Son, whom I love; with you I am well pleased" (Luke 3:22). It was from this life-giving place in the center of his soul that Jesus moved into his work with the understanding that he was already seen and approved by his Father. He didn't have to *do* anything to achieve life in his soul.

It's a good thing this life-giving relationship was in place because, just after this affirmation, Jesus quickly found himself in a time when his human relationships could not help him. He was alone in the wilderness for forty days with only this connection to help him withstand intense physical and spiritual hunger as Satan challenged his identity as the Son of God and his Father's character and plans for his life (Luke 4:3, 7). But Jesus's trust in his Father was solid in the center, so he survived the extreme circumstances with integrity. Later, as Jesus began to teach, lead, and heal—constantly giving to others—the Source within him provided an unending spiritual supply even at the times he had to physically and emotionally recharge through time alone in prayer: "Jesus went out to a mountainside to pray, and spent the night praying to God" (Luke 6:12). This mysterious, ever-flowing, central connection to God was so strong and trusted by Jesus that it proved itself immovable even in his darkest moment, when he knew the cross was imminent: "He fell with his face to the ground and prayed, 'My Father, if it is possible, may this cup be taken from me. Yet not as I will, but as you will'" (Matt. 26:39). It was the connection to his Father at the center of his soul that enabled him to face this moment, even while knowing death itself was coming.

And I struggle to grasp this connection even under the best circumstances!

The sustaining life of God was lodged at the center of Jesus. The original design for all people was a state of intimacy with God at the very center of human life. In the beginning, humans received the life of God in a personal way as he "breathed into his nostrils the breath of life, and the man became a living being" (Gen. 2:7). God then placed them in the environment of Eden that supported living in relationship together. People were made for a life-giving, life-sustaining connection with a divine God; your human relationships were never meant to play this role. Your core, circle, comrades, communities, and crowds are a critical part of God's design for your thriving human life, but he is the only Source made to reach into the very center of your soul. Because of this design, God is the necessary and primary foundation of every other relationship in your life. Whatever you don't receive first from your heavenly Father through relationship with Christ, you will warp your human relationships trying to find. Putting your family and friendships in the center of your blueprint will always fail because they don't belong in that space. You are invited to be filled from the center with true, eternal belonging. When you accept Jesus into that place, you will free your attachments to change, grow, ebb, and flow around this immovable interior. You will approach others already certain that you are known, included, welcomed, encouraged, and expectantly connected to the One who is able to quench all these thirsts.

Jesus referred to this as "living water."

He used those words the day he met a Samaritan woman, who was a lot like you and me, at a well. She had looked for connection with someone who could save her life in a place where she felt constantly deficient. She desperately wanted to belong with a husband but repeatedly came up short: she was on her sixth man after having had five previous husbands. There is an interesting scholarly debate about what caused her to have so many past husbands. Some assume she just slept around, marrying them in succession. Given the culture around her, many find this unlikely and believe she may actually have been abandoned by these men because of some sort of flaw—perhaps being unable to conceive a child, which would have been seen as the primary duty of being a wife. Whatever was lacking, it prompted a disappointing search for ultimate belonging with man after man. On the day Jesus encountered her it was clear her search for the satisfaction of her soul had come up short again. They both knew she was at rock bottom.

Jesus asked her for a drink and, surprised, she pushed back on his countercultural request. (She was not a Jew! And she was a woman!) Jesus said to her, "If you knew the gift of God and who it is that asks you for a drink, you would have asked him and he would have given you **living water**" (John 4:10, emphasis added). This term was also a reference to the actual well beside them. "Living waters" were the groundwaters that came up through the center of the well, filling it from underneath so that water could be drawn out and thirst could be quenched. Without living waters, the well would be dry and useless, unable to sustain life. By choosing these words, Jesus pointed to a deeper source for the life of her soul that would never run dry. He spoke into the thirst he knew was inside this woman that had driven her to search for life in man after man. Jesus offered her a better source—a power to quench her thirst far beyond the well that had run dry. He spoke through the physical realm, into her spiritual condition when he said:

> Everyone who drinks this water will be thirsty again, but whoever drinks the water I give them will never thirst. Indeed, the water I give them will become in them a spring of water welling up to eternal life. (John 4:13–14)

A spring that never runs dry! A spring that somehow is connected to a never-ending life that satisfies your perpetual, internal, invisible thirst! The same kind of thirst that sent me searching for life through my career and work. The same one that sent this woman to man after man. She was especially shocked at Jesus's mention of including her in this eternal life: she was a Samaritan, and the Jews claimed eternal life was only available through their covenant with their God, a covenant she was excluded from. Yet Jesus's words promised a new source available also to *her*. Whatever he meant by "living water," it had to mean something that could flow within even a Samaritan woman, quenching every thirst that she tried to satisfy through men. She could be filled in an unseen place at the center of her life. The arguably even bigger news was that if this woman—an outcast to the Jews and her own people, with broken relationships and at rock bottom—could drink from this Source, then surely it was available to everyone!

That's exactly what Jesus was saying. You can ask God right now to fill you up with it.

Connection to the Source

Jesus was fully alive, but we—at best—enjoy fleeting moments or briefly connected experiences with God. His offer of living water can restore and strengthen the intended connection that humanity was created to enjoy uninterrupted with our Creator. The bond was originally broken by the sin of Adam and Eve, but it was restored in and through Jesus, who did not sin, and so he was made an acceptable offering for you at his death on a cross. He reestablished the possibility of your connection to the Father that Adam lost when he went looking for life elsewhere. This redemption is only possible because that same sin in your life has been dealt with at the cross.

The cross is where you reconnect to the Source.

You belong with Jesus. But you were born into disconnection, the same kind Adam felt when he was banished from Eden. The cross represents the ultimate cost of the distance created by sin—but you don't have to endure it because Jesus went in your place. Jesus took on your alienation to win back the intimacy with God you were created for. You can be at home with God instead of living in perpetual loneliness. The cross is your connection point. The cross is where your sin was dealt with and the barrier between you and God was destroyed. The cross is the place where what's broken gets repaired. The cross is where your soul comes back to life because Jesus triumphed over death's power. The cross gives you access to the Source that will overwhelm any kind of death with life.

> We were therefore buried with him through baptism into death in order that, just as Christ was raised from the dead through the glory of the Father, we too may live a new life.
> For if we have been united with him in a death like his, we will certainly also be united with him in a resurrection like his. (Rom. 6:4–5)

When you become new in Christ, you die with Jesus on the cross and are resurrected into a new life of connection with the Source, a life that will never end. This Source connects you to a God who sees and knows you, who includes you, who welcomes you, who sends you encouragement, and who births a hope in you for new possibilities. That's where you belong. The unending life of your soul begins when you join Jesus in his death and resurrection. (This is exactly what baptism symbolizes!) When you receive Jesus as Lord and Savior, the disconnection from God is over and you receive the Source to dwell with you and live in you: his name is the Holy Spirit. The Spirit who brings life takes up residence at your center to not only fill you but also equip you to function in life-giving human relationships. Jesus flourished in earthly relationships according to God's design for his soul, and he is offering his Spirit to do the same for you.

Once you receive the forgiveness and reconciliation of Christ, the Holy Spirit seals you with his presence, slowly remaking your mind and heart as he fills you up. He teaches you to see yourself and others clearly, correcting misunderstandings about your identity and self-worth that drive you to others for affirmation. He connects you to people—from your core to your crowds—who help grow and nourish you every day. He teaches you how to tell the truth and love well in all these realms of relationship. Living connected to the Source will reorder your relational world because you no longer look to people for your primary source of belonging. You know where you belong, and the Spirit settles your mind and heart on him in your search

> **Living connected to the Source will reorder your relational world because you no longer look to people for your primary source of belonging.**

for that home. The Father, Son, and Holy Spirit invite you to share in their life-giving triune connection at the deepest point of your humanity—the center of you, your soul created by him. This connection reestablishes healthy patterns of relationship in your life from the inside out:

In your core. . .

The Holy Spirit reassures you of the unconditional love of a Father who fully sees and knows you. Jesus offered this love to his **core** of Peter, James, and John, never expecting perfection in return. **With the Spirit in the center, you can also live seen, known, and loved completely.** This trust equips you with the courage to love your core unconditionally, accepting their flaws and showing them yours with no hiding or shame because you already have full and free acceptance in Christ.

In your circle. . .

The Spirit invites you into the **circle** of God to walk in daily friendship with him. Jesus changed the world by

189

making twelve friends and inviting them into his daily life with God. **With the Spirit in the center, you have a friend who always includes you in what he is doing.** Friendship with Jesus means you walk and work together, shoulder to shoulder. As Jesus lifts your burdens, you have the capacity and strength to do the same for your own circle of friends without fear or selfishness, in the warmth of true friendship.

In your comrades. . .

The Spirit bonds you to **comrades** who will fight with you on the battlefield. Jesus had seventy-two kingdom comrades, training and equipping them to expand the kingdom of God and spread the gospel. Jesus enlists *you* to become part of the plan for the defeat of his enemy. **With the Spirit in the center, you sustain passion for a fight with eternal meaning** and give your life for fellow soldiers who have your back on a common mission.

In your community. . .

The Spirit is the glue of an eternal **community** spanning all eras and geographies. Jesus walked on earth with simultaneous belonging in a heavenly community in his eternal home. **With the Spirit in the center, you are welcomed into his community with heavenly support and provision.** You are free to give and receive generous provision with no strings attached because your Father's resources are at your disposal.

In the crowd. . .

God can use you to impact eternity with just a whisper in a **crowd**. Jesus lived with purpose, hope, and compassion, unafraid to step into the unknown and see what his Father wanted to do there. **With the Spirit in the center, you live**

expectant that he is always at work. Kingdom impact is a possibility any place on any day, bringing life to your soul.

I've caught glimpses of beautiful moments of connection with Jesus that fill me with the sense that I am being sustained by this living water. The experience of the Spirit sometimes feels like a sudden sense of security and belonging that overtakes me. The truth is I always am with him, but sometimes I experience that and sometimes I forget. I was reminded of the strength in my center in the spring of 2020, a few weeks into the Covid stay-at-home orders, around the time people started to freak out from the isolation. Everyone was discovering their human connections sustained much more of their life than previously imagined, and our sense of belonging was taking a big hit. With a sprinkle of fear on top of the isolation, many people's mental and emotional health was shredding, and we all understood why.

One afternoon I was out on a run by myself, thinking about the stunted relationships and ruined plans, when I had a sudden rush of realization. Despite the scarcity, I was actually doing okay. No, I wasn't pleased with the state of my life and connections. Yes, I missed having the nourishing contact I needed. I had many points of stress and sorrow—*but!*—I felt stable in a way I didn't expect, in a way I shouldn't have. On that run I appreciated my center connection with God in a new way: I knew the only reason I was staying solid in these awful circumstances was because of the Spirit of God himself. I had a well inside me that I usually overlooked. On that run I experienced a rush of the living water that was filling me up in all these terribly dry places.

As I think back on that period early in the pandemic, I see how we all suffered for the lack of human connection:

as souls we need more relational contact than we were allowed. None of us thrived in a state of separation because—as God declared in the beginning—it's not good for humans to be alone. However, that day on the run I felt the strength of a relationship in my center when most of my others were stripped away. There seemed to be life flowing from him in the middle of myself—the middle of my soul—that wasn't running dry despite everything around me turning to dust. It was my biggest gift during that terrible time: the ability to see just how life-sustaining Jesus truly is. I had my low moments during the spring and summer of 2020, but I walked away with something I otherwise may have missed: my dire need for a heavenly Source in the center of my soul—and his sufficiency and willingness to be just that.

There are still moments or seasons when I feel more or less connected to God. I know even my times of connection don't come close to the constant state of belonging in which Jesus lived. Luckily, wherever your connection with God is today, you are invited to deepen your reliance on the Source of life. You can take a deeper drink from the living water. Jesus called that process learning to "abide" more fully in him. Increasingly abiding in Christ deepens the quality, time, and intensity of our relationship with the Father, which benefits all our relationships here on earth as well. Jesus describes it like the connection of a branch to a vine that is ultimately tended by a gardener.

> I am the true vine, and my Father is the gardener. . . . Remain in me, as I also remain in you. No branch can bear fruit by itself; it must remain in the vine. Neither can you bear fruit unless you remain in me. (John 15:1, 4)

When you abide in Christ, your soul is completely provided for and perfectly loved in all the ways you need. You can bear more and more fruit in your human connections as you naturally realign, reprioritize, and redesign the way you approach them. This nourishment from the vine means you can stop trying to take what you need from other people and instead receive life from God. You can start sharing that life with others—your friends, family, and even strangers. People *are* critical to a full, thriving human life within God's design, but *Jesus* is meant to be at the center of our human existence, connecting us to a Father through his Spirit who can enable us to truly love others out of the deep water in our soul.

Love from the Source

When you have a connection to God in your center, you become freer and freer to love others. A relationship with Jesus means you can belong in all kinds of relationships without depending upon them for your ultimate sense of belonging.

> You, my brothers and sisters, were called to be free. But do not use your freedom to indulge the flesh; rather, serve one another humbly in love. For the entire law is fulfilled in keeping this one command: "Love your neighbor as yourself." (Gal. 5:13–14)

Jesus felt absolutely free to interact with his neighbors in whatever way was needed. He wasn't using them to fill himself up, so he was free to embody perfect *love* in all its different forms. Love is patient and kind. It doesn't dishonor others. Love doesn't seek what's good for itself or easiest in the moment. Love isn't proud or angry or jealous; instead, love freely forgives, gives, and receives. Love rejects evil, never covering for it or calling it good or approving of it. Love tells the truth. Love looks and acts all kinds of different ways, from your core into the crowds. Jesus was sometimes gentle and inviting and sometimes firm, even rebuking. He included generously and also drew lines and set boundaries. He called people out and invited people in. He simply was free to do, say, and act in a way that showed every person around him how much they were worth to God. He did what was required to ascribe worth to another person, even if it cost him something in the process. He could do this because the Source at his center was always renewing and filling and providing.

We all get the character of his love wrong sometimes: we add to it or take away from it. You and I learned to love in imperfect families and situations, so the way we love isn't perfect. I grew up in an environment where I learned the falsehood that loving others means being agreeable and striving to avoid causing others discomfort. I witnessed behavior that told me that love doesn't always tell the truth if you can spare someone's feelings. I grew up confused about the relationship between love and emotions and between love and truth. I carried confusion about the difference between kindness and politeness. I thought I always needed to prioritize keeping the peace over asking for accountability or justice. The things I mistook for love were instead slightly twisted versions of it taught by imperfect people loving the best ways they could, looking to plug holes in their own human souls. Most of us try earnestly to love others, but we are born disconnected from the Source itself who *is* love. So we fall short, even on our best days.

Jesus offers us the chance for a growing connection that will begin to fill us in our center, teaching us how to love according to the Spirit of God. He didn't love everyone by the same methods and in the same ways, but he loved everyone all the time. He showed us what love looks and acts like in these five different kinds of relationships when you aren't looking to fill yourself but are free to fill others through an experience with the love of God. The Spirit of God pours love into your center.

> God's love has been poured out into our hearts through the Holy Spirit, who has been given to us. (Rom. 5:5)

Jesus didn't invite every comrade into his twelve, but he loved them. Jesus didn't take his twelve everywhere he took his core three, but he loved them. Jesus interacted with people in the crowd he never laid eyes on again, but he loved them. If I apply this thinking to my own life, I've got to admit it makes sense: I wouldn't want my husband's coworker or my distant aunt to love me as they love a best friend or their own child. That would be weird. Love behaves differently in various relational spaces but is no less impactful. Being connected to the Source means you're *equipped* to love everyone you come across and *free* not to love everyone the same way.

Being connected to the Source means you're *equipped* to love everyone you come across and *free* not to love everyone the same way.

From your core to your crowds, people will have all different levels of access to a relationship with you. The life of Christ shows us that it is okay for love to look different for different people in different spaces with different kinds of relationships.

The command to "love your neighbor as yourself" used to feel to me as though Jesus wanted me to "love every person the way I love my best friend." But this is not what we see in Jesus's life at all. Not only has this misunderstanding made me feel like a failure at loving others, but the result is that I have devalued what I deem "smaller" chances to love someone. I have mistakenly thought that any relationship I offer someone that is "less" than my core is ultimately insufficient or less important. This is a trap! It will keep you from so many chances to love. God is putting all kinds of people in your path; you just need as robust a relational world and definition of love as Jesus had.

Love could be as simple as looking a stranger in the face with a warm smile instead of ignoring them while you snap someone in the Starbucks line. It might be telling the truth when you're asked a question instead of making an excuse. It might be giving up your plans to go help a friend or giving money to someone's new business start-up. Love isn't one thing to one kind of person. Love acknowledges different possibilities in different relationships and is comfortable with the idea that God can keep loving them even if you will never see them again. Your warm attention in the coffee line might be the most you can do to love them, and if so, it is enough.

Certain kinds of connections feel challenging to each one of us. You might find it easy to trust a core but harder to commit to the daily contact of friendship in a circle. You might find it fun or invigorating to interact with strangers in a crowd but shy away from the accountability and teamwork of having comrades. Certain kinds of relationships are tough because, well, we have issues. These issues tend to sit in the places in our souls where we struggle to let *God* in. Because of our past, our personalities, or our problems, we aren't completely filled with his life even when we want to connect to the Source, so the struggle is real to build healthy relationships with others. It's a journey for all of us toward a life of deeper connection and a more vibrant life.

Read through these words from Scripture and choose a verse that speaks to you in the realm you experience the most relational issues. Even circle it right here on the page and ask God to become the Source that flows through every room in the blueprint of your soul.

- If you struggle to believe God knows you and to let him into the depth of your **core**, memorize Psalm 139:1–3:

> You have searched me, LORD,
>   and you know me.
> You know when I sit and when I rise;
>   you perceive my thoughts from afar.
> You discern my going out and my lying down;
>   you are familiar with all my ways.

- If you struggle to believe God is a friend, walking with you as in a **circle**, memorize John 15:15:

> I no longer call you servants, because a servant does not know his master's business. Instead, I have called you friends, for everything that I learned from my Father I have made known to you.

- If you struggle to feel part of a God-given mission in solidarity with **comrades**, memorize Matthew 28:18–20:

> All authority in heaven and on earth has been given to me. Therefore go and make disciples of all nations, baptizing them in the name of the Father and of the Son and of the Holy Spirit, and teaching them to obey everything I have commanded you. And surely I am with you always, to the very end of the age.

- If you struggle to see how the **community** you've gathered is connected to where God is leading you, memorize Romans 8:28:

> And we know that in all things God works for the good of those who love him, who have been called according to his purpose.

- If life following Jesus feels boring or stale, never piquing your curiosity in a **crowd**, memorize John 3:8:

> The wind blows wherever it pleases. You hear its sound, but you cannot tell where it comes from or where it is going. So it is with everyone born of the Spirit.

You were made to be filled with the truth and grace of God in all these relational spaces. There is a blueprint for the belonging you were made to experience.

Now that you've thought about all your connections with God and others, it's time to put it all together. In the next chapter you will use the same blueprint found in the life of Jesus to look at all your relationships. You are going to look at all the names of the people you've been thinking about and put it all back together into one design. As you put pen to paper and talk to God about all your people, consider where changes to the design of your relational world can help you live life to the fullest. I believe the Holy Spirit has been and will be at work helping you shift, adjust, and grow into new spaces on your blueprint where a deeper sense of belonging awaits.

Your Redesign

As I have loved you, so you must love one another.

John 13:34

Jesus is helping me redesign part of my relational world. His invitation came a year or two ago in the form of a persistent prayer—one I couldn't shake off even when I told myself I was fine. The prayer I constantly returned to was, "God, will you help me develop a circle?" Asking for God's help with this was different from moments I've made well-intentioned promises to "live more like Jesus." Anytime I've done that I've fallen short, no matter how good my intentions. This prayer was more of a childlike request from someone who didn't know how to begin. It kept popping up during my prolonged and personal experience of loneliness. Some days it didn't matter, and I didn't pray the prayer for a while. But it just wouldn't leave.

God was opening a window for change in my life, *inviting me* to something better. I believe he is going to do the same for you. It might start with new language or a simple awareness of something you hadn't seen before. When I first prayed that simple prayer, the loneliness that stems from a missing circle was obvious in my life. But the language of this blueprint design gave me words for the small nagging emptiness I felt after working by myself all week, or when I yearned to talk with a friend about what I was reading, or when I couldn't find a buddy for a weekday run, or when I realized I wasn't mentoring any younger women the way I used to do. The blueprint helped me see and name the realm of belonging I was craving *and* start to acknowledge the ongoing choices it was going to take for me to regain the sense of belonging I lacked.

This blueprint of relationships in Jesus's life is the key to combatting whatever kind of loneliness you've come to think of as "normal." A thoughtful redesign of your relational world could offer you the chance to give and receive more life-giving love, friendship, support, and purpose from the center of your being all the way out into the crowds. A redesign of your relationships is possible; the question is, even if you see the destination, where do you begin?

I began with a decision to work on a team again. I felt a sense in prayer that God was pressing on my desire to work alone. Even though I loved the flexibility of schedule it gave me, I knew it was a key piece of the demise of my circle. I felt tension on this issue for over a year until I got the chance to make a change. I was still hesitant to give

Your Redesign

up what I liked about my situation, but the opportunity seemed to be an invitation from God into more life. Would I trust him?

When I said yes to a change in my work situation, I was not at all sure it was the right one. But very quickly it opened up new relationships and put me in proximity of potential circle friendships as I worked shoulder to shoulder with others again. The building of true friendship will take time. No hole in your blueprint will have a quick fix. A circle won't be created in my life with one decision, but one decision was necessary to begin the shift. It also won't come without cost: I have definitely sacrificed some freedom in my work that I had enjoyed. As I said in the beginning of this book, relationships are a long and messy business, but they also have the power to exponentially increase the vitality of your life, both internally and externally. I am continuing to try to say yes to growing a circle, trusting that the blueprint found in the life of Jesus will be best for my life as well—even when the opportunities to create this space in my relational world aren't always things I would choose!

About six months after starting to pray for a stronger circle, my closest friend moved away. It really knocked the wind out of me. I truly grieved this change. For many weeks, I'd suddenly begin to cry, unable to stop the tears. She was such an important part of my daily and weekly rhythms and of my heart as someone deep in my core. I was keenly aware that my circle was already too small, so I sarcastically said to God, "Thanks a lot for taking someone away at the very moment I was asking you for *more* friends." It dawned on me over the following months that God's work to build my relational world isn't linear. I considered whether God

203

would actually work through this loss as part of the answer to my prayer for a better circle. Only *he* can see how all the pieces of my life fit together to impact my soul. After my friend's departure I did push myself to say yes to invitations and spend time with other friends that I'd reserved for only her in the past. The pain over losing my deepest daily connection, I must admit, has undoubtedly played a role in the development of a more robust circle, though the pain of loss is most certainly not the method I'd have chosen.

God is never predictable in the way he grows us! Whatever prayer you begin to pray about your relationships may lead you down a road you didn't expect, but he cares deeply about how your relationships are functioning. You can trust him even if redesigning your relational world doesn't happen in clear bullet points or straight lines. He wants you to experience true belonging. The loneliness, loss, or lack you feel now is not his desire for your life. Jesus stated his intention for us clearly when he said, "The thief comes only to steal and kill and destroy; I have come that they may have life, and have it to the full" (John 10:10). He wants to invite you into relationships that are full of life.

Reimagining and reconstructing those connections, however, is likely to be a longer, slower work than you might choose. I have had to question the ways I was pursuing relationships in my past and try to trust that the life I see Jesus living in the pages of Scripture will bring me greater fullness than my own ways. I still have a lot of room to grow more thriving relationships. I still have past pain and hurt in my way, and I still experience waves of loneliness. The difference now is that I can see a better design, and I am watching expectantly for God to offer me the chance to move in that direction. I believe he wants a thriving relational world for me even more than I do.

Nearly everyone I know would agree they could probably be more purposeful or thoughtful about their relationships. So that's what we are about to do with a pen and paper. And the blueprint Jesus left for you. You can use your blueprint to engage God, watching for where he may want to begin. As you think and pray about how your relationships are constructed, I hope you will trust that God truly is *for* you and that he has at least one small way you could start now to better align your relationships with the life Jesus lived. I pray this prayer for your life to be more full of the love of God because of what he shows you in the next few pages:

> I pray that you, being rooted and established in love, may have power, together with all the Lord's holy people, to grasp how wide and long and high and deep is the love of Christ, and to know this love that surpasses knowledge— that you may be filled to the measure of all the fullness of God.
>
> Now to him who is able to do immeasurably more than all we ask or imagine, according to his power that is at work within us, to him be glory in the church and in Christ Jesus throughout all generations, for ever and ever! Amen. (Eph. 3:17–21)

God knows the way out of loneliness into belonging and connection. Ask and imagine something good and new for yourself, knowing he has the power to do far more than that!

Now, let's put the full blueprint together in one big picture.

The Blueprint

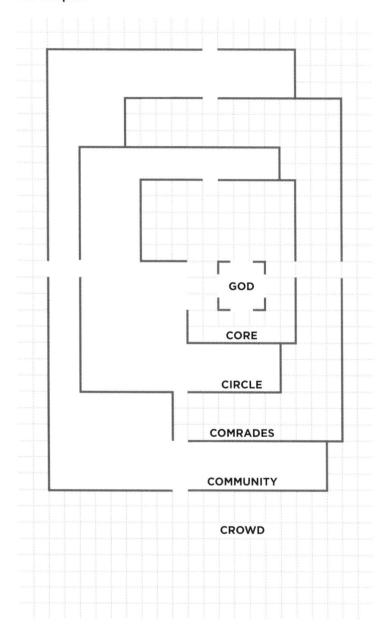

GOD

CORE

CIRCLE

COMRADES

COMMUNITY

CROWD

This blueprint of Jesus's five different types of relationships is exactly that: *a blueprint.* I like the word *blueprint* because constructing one is a creative process. Jesus's life isn't a rigid plan for precise duplication. Use his blueprint to dream up with God something new for your relationships. You can start from where you are and reimagine your relational world with his in mind. A blueprint is a building plan, a picture of where you're headed. Jesus had different people, different factors, a different culture, and a different starting point than you do. The original lines are in different places for you, but you can use it as an overlay for your current life.

Your first job with this blueprint is simple: add in the names. Go back to the end of each chapter: who did you think of for each realm of relationship? Transfer the names to each part of the blueprint. As you work through the blueprint, here's a reminder of the essence of the five different parts of the design:

Center: Is Jesus there? If not, wrestle with who Jesus is and what his life, death, and resurrection mean for you. Receive the gospel of repentance and forgiveness from sin and new life through his Spirit so all your relationships can thrive from the inside out.

Core (one to three names): Your unconditional few.

Circle (five to ten names): Your people: the ones you live life with, working, playing, and seeing weekly.

Comrades (Jesus had over seventy): These people share a common mission and passion in your life but with less access and regular activity than a circle.

Community: (as many as you've got): The people whose doors you can knock on around the world and be welcome. You are truly connected but don't share a focused, common mission.

Crowds: Name your crowds by the places of likely encounter ("people at my gym," "parents at my kid's softball games," etc.).

Mess with the lines a little. Consider your current structure. Sketch out the part you want to rebuild. As you do this, give yourself lots of permission to change your mind, redraw lines, and make it messy. Mine always has names on the line between layers or in the open doorways if someone falls between rooms. I put question marks by names I need to think or pray about. I put arrows in either direction to indicate whether someone is moving closer or further away from where they are right now. Your relational world is not static; this is just a snapshot!

Jesus may have lived perfectly within his Father's design for human relationships, but he also grew in the wisdom he needed over time. You can do the same. Just begin conversations with God about what your relational world can look like as you expand, grow, and build upon where you are now. Maybe you will find a specific new prayer to start praying just like I did.

As you consider your blueprint full of names, use these prompts:

Single biggest takeaway from your blueprint:

A surprise insight:

A relief you feel:

Something you love about what you see:

Something you know you need to change:

The room on the blueprint you feel most comfortable in:

The room you avoid:

The room you've often struggled to develop:

The room you need to spend more time in:

The room that is most connected to feelings of loneliness:

The room you need to spend less time in:

The room you need to invest more/less money in:

Challenge you most need God's help to address:

Your biggest prayer as you look over your whole blueprint:

As you ask and imagine, be confident that God has even more in store for you! The Spirit of God can reveal the next step into greater belonging for you from here. I believe he has a unique, heavenly design for your life here on earth. I hope you will keep this blueprint, change it over time, and pray over it frequently. On the following pages there are more empty blueprints so you can return and reconsider as life and relationships shift.

This blueprint is the beginning of better connection. It's a tool for language and awareness that you and God can consider together; it is not your whole journey. The journey is lifelong because relationships will always be essential to the life of your soul. I hope your messy sketch of a redesigned relational world will give you the courage you need to walk away from loneliness and accept God's invitation to life and growth. Jesus has an abundant life to offer you through rich, deep, layered human connection. And he remains the one at the center with the power to truly turn this into your blueprint for belonging.

ACKNOWLEDGMENTS

The writing of this book truly began on the day that Jesus revealed to me that I belonged with him. At my worst, he received me and flooded my life with the overwhelming truth that I always have and always will belong to him. He is the powerful source of belonging that has sustained me more times than I can count when I have been lonely in all kinds of ways. "Thank you" isn't a big enough phrase for the gratitude I feel to Jesus for counting me one of his own. I see his generosity and grace to me in the core, circle, comrades, and community he has given me in which to belong. Thank you to the people who show me all the time what it feels like to be known, included, encouraged, welcomed, and expectant, especially my husband, Bill, and my kids, Andrew, Luke, Zoe, and Hope, to whom this book is dedicated.

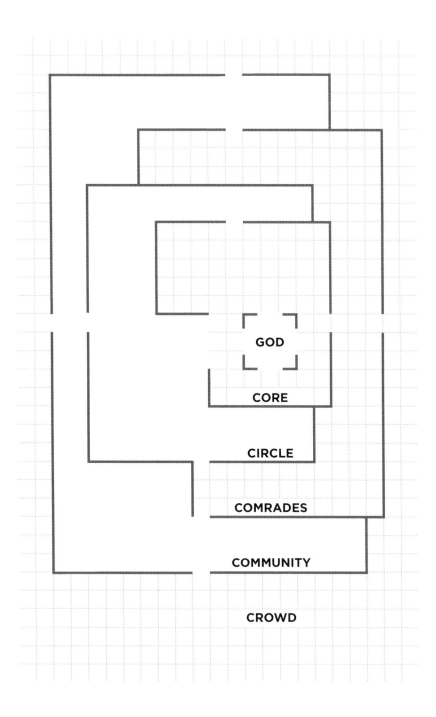

GOD

CORE

CIRCLE

COMRADES

COMMUNITY

CROWD

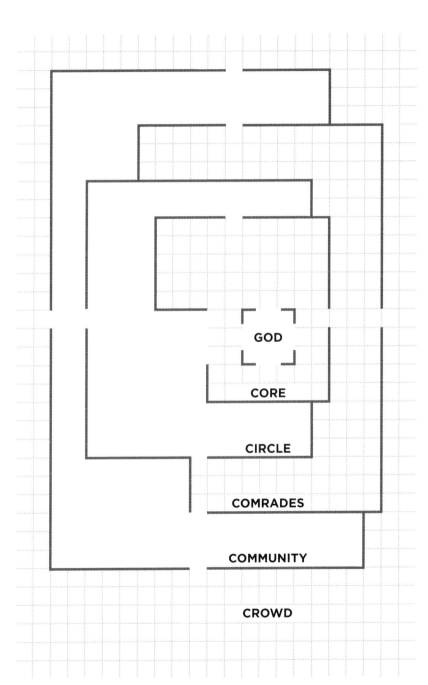

GOD

CORE

CIRCLE

COMRADES

COMMUNITY

CROWD

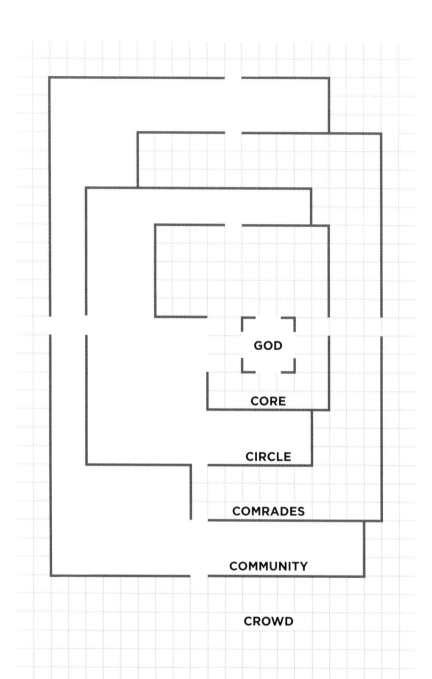

GOD

CORE

CIRCLE

COMRADES

COMMUNITY

CROWD

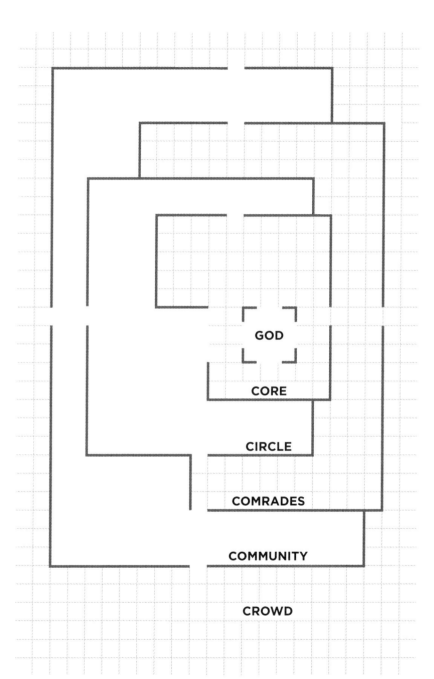

GOD

CORE

CIRCLE

COMRADES

COMMUNITY

CROWD

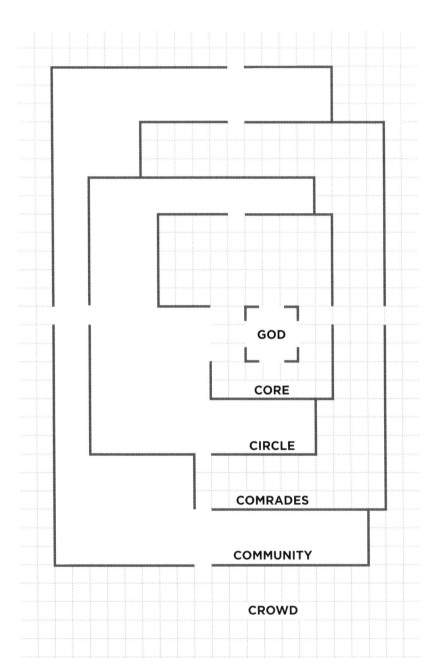

GOD

CORE

CIRCLE

COMRADES

COMMUNITY

CROWD

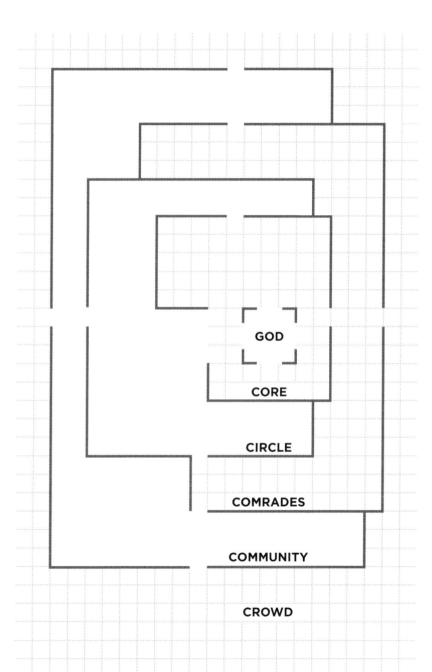

GOD

CORE

CIRCLE

COMRADES

COMMUNITY

CROWD

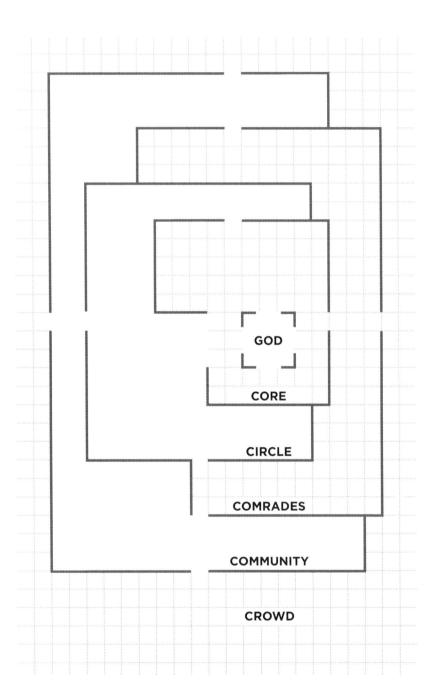

GOD

CORE

CIRCLE

COMRADES

COMMUNITY

CROWD

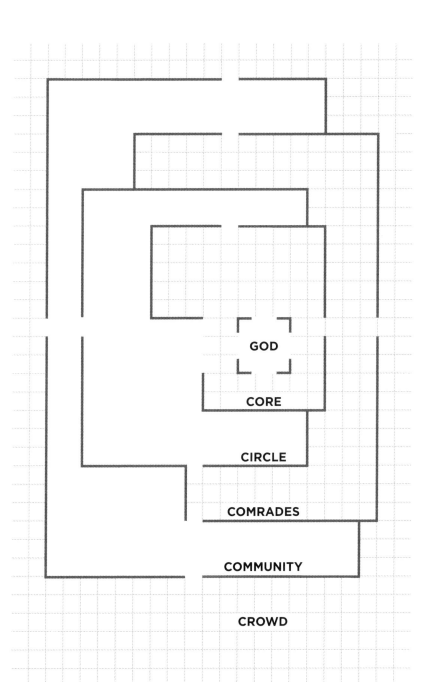

GOD

CORE

CIRCLE

COMRADES

COMMUNITY

CROWD

ALLI PATTERSON is passionate about helping others build a life on the firm foundation of Jesus's truth and grace. She holds a master's degree in biblical studies from Dallas Theological Seminary and is a teaching pastor at Crossroads Church. She lives with her husband, Bill, their four children, and one very bratty cat. Learn more at TheAlliPatterson.com.